Excluded from School:
Complex discourses and psychological perspectives

Excluded from School:
Complex discourses and psychological perspectives

Christopher Arnold, Jane Yeomans
and Sarah Simpson
with a chapter by Mike Solomon

Trentham Books
Stoke on Trent, UK and Sterling, USA

Trentham Books Limited
Westview House   22883 Quicksilver Drive
734 London Road   Sterling
Oakhill   VA 20166-2012
Stoke on Trent   USA
Staffordshire
England ST4 5NP

© 2009 Christopher Arnold, Jane Yeomans and Sarah Simpson

First published 2009

British Library Cataloguing-in-Publication Data
A catalogue record for this book is available from the British Library

ISBN: 978 1 85856 439 5

Designed and typeset by Trentham Print Design Ltd, Chester and printed in Great Britain by Page Bros (Norwich) Ltd, Norfolk.

Contents

Acknowledgments

Inevitably a book of this nature involves many more people than those credited as authors.

The authors are extremely grateful to colleagues and friends in Sandwell's Inclusion Support Service under the leadership of Andy Gravenstede, the Principal Educational Psychologist. The case examples have been compiled through the patience and assistance of many parents, young people, staff working in schools, pupil referral units and other agencies such as Parent Partnership Services and Social Inclusion. We have benefited from the extremely helpful comments of many who have read earlier versions of the text, notably Nick Jarman, Marie Fitzer and particularly Sylvia Coury whose attention to detail helped iron out many discrepancies, although the authors accept full responsibility for any errors or omissions.

Finally, we thank our partners and families for their patience.

Dedication:
To all the young people, families and staff affected by exclusion from school

About the authors

Dr Christopher Arnold is a Senior Educational Psychologist working for Sandwell M.B.C. Along with Jane Yeomans he has written *Psychology for Teaching Assistants*, Trentham (2005) and *Teaching Learning and Psychology,* David Fulton (2006). He has written numerous articles and his work has been featured in the *Times, Times Educational Supplement, Guardian, Daily Mail,* BBC Radio 5 live and many local radio stations.

Dr Jane Yeomans is a Specialist Senior Educational Psychologist working for Sandwell MBC. She is also seconded to the University of Birmingham as an Academic and Professional Tutor for the initial training and post qualification doctoral programmes in Educational Psychology. She was previously a Primary and Special School teacher, including working as a SENCo in two inner city schools in Birmingham. Along with Christopher Arnold she has written *Psychology for Teaching Assistants* and *Teaching Learning and Psychology.*

Dr Sarah Simpson is a Clinical Psychologist seconded from CAMHS into Sandwell MBC. She works within a residential facility for children with emotional and behavioural difficulties, and also provides training and consultation to various agencies regarding emotional health and wellbeing within educational settings.

Dr Mike Solomon is a Consultant Clinical Psychologist at the Tavistock Clinic, London, and the London Borough of Camden Secondary Behaviour Support Service. He works in a Pupil Referral Unit, and also provides training in mental health for education professionals, as well as offering consultancy to schools and education services. He has spoken at national and international conferences about mental health in education and the dynamics of inclusion and exclusion.

PART 1
Context and Scope

Introduction to Part One

Exclusion, expulsion, imprisonment, transportation, removal, incarceration, internment, exiling, time out, expatriation, ostracism, banishment, ethnic cleansing, genocide, apartheid and ultimately, execution or judicial capital punishment have all been used as methods of social control. Whatever the term, they share *separation* as social tool. There are basic biological and evolutionary processes that might account for this type of behaviour. Loehle (1995), for example, describes the biological perspective for social avoidance. Behavioural mechanisms are important for reducing the incidence of disease. If an animal looks diseased it would be in the interests of the remaining group to isolate the individual to avoid transmission of the disease. It is also in the interests of the sick individual to isolate itself to avoid the dangers of contracting additional disease so that their immune system can concentrate on fighting the current sickness. Organisms which are capable of perceiving sickness in individuals are likely to display such adaptive behaviour.

Individuals with differences or disabilities have always been part of a society or culture. Throughout history there have been different ways of responding to these differences. Written records of treatments for disorders and disabilities go back to Greek and Roman times. Disabilities were attributed to Gods or other superhuman beings who possessed magical powers. Madness or behavioural disorder was a punishment by a deity for the sins of the individual or sins passed down from the parents.

In Western European society, the Christian Church took a significant role in the care of the disabled and insane. By the fourth century AD, monasteries had developed with a strict discipline of ritual and routine designed to facilitate moral perfection through asceticism. Two to three centuries later, their inhabitants became powerful forces for civilisation through literacy and scholarship. The cloisters of these institutions became natural places to pro-

3

tect the vulnerable from the outside world. Institutionalisation of the insane and otherwise vulnerable was born.

Today we may judge institutionalisation harshly, but in the context of the time, perhaps it should be viewed more kindly. Hardship and death were alternative fates for those not able to function in a disordered society.

During the Renaissance, one driving force was a recognition that the ancient worlds of Greece and Rome had a quality of civilisation and art not yet restored in the fourteenth to sixteenth centuries. Rediscovery of old wisdom was a widespread aim. This led to experimentation in many fields, including anatomy. In the sixteenth century this included the dissection of the ear. The deaf and blind were found to be able to reason if provided with the means to access the information. The tide was turning on the belief that disability was the work of the devil.

The development of printing presses led to widespread access to books. Information was spread through the printed word. One consequence was that the earlier discovery of using pieces of curved glass to enhance poor eyesight became more widely known. By the sixteenth century reading glasses were common in Italy and people who were previously deemed blind gained some access to improved vision. In the enlightened city state of Venice we find large scale public institutions established for the disabled and sick (Arnold and Baldouf-Burdes, 2002).

The fates of those with difficult behaviour were, however, less favourable. Lunatic hospitals existed more for the protection of society than the well-being of the user and were described as 'asylums'. Descriptions of people deemed insane (and therefore suited for incarceration) included: 'mentally retarded, aged, deranged, albinos and epileptics', but usage extended to 'dissenters, heretics and others causing disruption of social or religious order' (in Winzer, 1993). By the eighteenth century the attribution of behavioural difference to demoniac possession was being questioned. Instead of demons, masturbation was blamed.

The age of the enlightenment saw the development of inductive science, with the use of reason rather than religion as a way of understanding and helping those with emotional and psychological difficulties. The Frenchman Pinel rejected the prevailing attributions for mental disorder (devil, witchcraft, the moon, libertanism, intoxicating liquor, masturbation) and outlined treatments based on sympathy and respect. Sufferers would have their manacles removed, receive regular visits and frequent conversations. Overall, they would be treated with kindness. The resulting reduction in the killing of wardens in the institutions gave the methods recognition and status. Unfortunately, Pinel was suspected of helping priests and emigrés and having some royalist sympathies so he lost his job, dying destitute. However the more humanitarian approach to difficult behaviour continued. The rise of the talking cures more associated with modern psychotherapy developed in the early to mid nineteenth century.

The work of Charcot, born in Paris in 1825, is worthy of note. Charcot became director of the first neurological clinic at Saltpière hospital in Paris. His main interest was the treatment of hysteria, which he believed to be caused by a weak neurological system perhaps damaged by an accident or trauma. He developed the use of hypnotism to study his patients, as he thought that hypnosis induced a mental state similar to hysteria. The actual treatment was not through hypnosis, but involved being cared for in special wards for patients of 'hystero-epilepsy'.

This treatment was challenged by one of his students, Babinski who suggested that the behaviour of sufferers actually arose from being placed in close proximity to patients with hysteria and epilepsy. The condition was exacerbated by staff who gave patients attention when these episodes occurred. At that time, hysterical episodes and fainting fits were not uncommon in boarding schools and other institutions. Babinski and Charcot devised a two stage approach to patients diagnosed with this condition. At first they would be removed from wards populated with others with the same condition and then suggestion would be used to implant different beliefs into the patients. The most effective approach seemed to be to ignore the hysterical behaviour and to suggest that the patient was now in recovery.

The role of schools

In 1870 both the UK and USA introduced compulsory education for all and special classes were created for children with various differences. In America there was a grade system which created a year-by-year curriculum and expected children to achieve certain levels of skill before moving to the next class. Additionally there were special classes for the ungraded, enabling the teacher to be freed of the external expectations. This also served to rid the majority of classes of unruly or otherwise difficult children. The descriptions from 1871 of children in America allocated to these classes reveal their function: '[to educate the] intellectually backward, incorrigibles, truants, low achievers'; (quoted by Hoffman, 1975 cited in Winzer, 1993).

The justification for a separation in education was simple:

Unreasonably disobedient and insubordinate youths who are a detriment to the good order and instruction of the school, are separated from it and placed here where they can be controlled and taught, without disturbing others. Truants, also, are placed in these schools for special discipline.

Children allocated to the special classes tended to leave education early to enter the work market, but legislation prohibiting child labour placed barriers to this. Children were expected to be in education longer and schools could not simply suggest that they had done all they could for them.

The theories or explanations of differences were being developed in the UK as well. The tripartite division of the mind distinguished between intellect (or intelligence), emotion and moral character. Those considered deficient in each category were commonly described as 'backward', 'unstable' and 'delinquent' respectively. Medical specialists began to distinguish between mental disorder or 'mere derangement of the intellect' to a different form, in which the intellect remained intact but morality was impaired. This was given the term 'moral insanity'.

Further distinctions were made according to the age of onset of the condition. *Moral defect* was set out by Dr Henry Maudsley, who suggested that moral insanity was not a useful term as it related to a loss of mind due to disease. Children, he argued, were defective in 'the common power of forming moral intuitions'. He suggested that the defect was inborn and therefore 'inherited or congenital'. In 1914 Tredgold went even further, suggesting that 'the condition is inborn ... and this ... causes them to be absolutely irreformable'. He suggested a genetic deficiency 'in the race the moral sense is the last to have been evolved; and it appears also to be the last to make its appearance in the individual' (Tredgold, 1914).

This interest in genetics (and eugenics) is found in Cyril Burt's treatise on *The Young Delinquent* (1927). Burt's thinking was reflected in British educational arrangements of the time and was very influential in shaping the way in which the system dealt with difference and diversity. He endorsed a range of educational provision. Special classes were organised and even special (intermediate) schools. Segregation under the Mental Deficiency Act was a frequent option, but for others, a guardian was allocated to act as a substitute for 'a parent too dull to love or control [the child]'. Hostels or residential homes provided a comfortable home, supervision and companionship. Teaching methods found in special schools were adopted to train in 'unskilled repetitive work, such as those of low intelligence can usually learn'.

Older boys were more commonly sent to Industrial Schools, in which vocational training was the main focus. These were mostly run by private companies and comments were made that the practices in these schools varied widely. There was a suggestion that they would be better run by Local Education Authorities. Segregation, exclusion or removal from the environment in which children behaved differently was still at the heart of intervention. The range of possible separations can still be found in modern systems.

The 1944 Education Act described different categories of children requiring special education. One category was the *maladjusted*. The definition was problematic as it depended on 'psychological disturbance' or 'emotional instability'. Specific training for teachers working in this field was not introduced until 1953 when the London Institute for Education (now the Institute for Education, University of London) established a course. The number of children attending schools providing specific (and exclusive) education for the *maladjusted* rose from 135 in 1947 to 1597 in 1960 and 7136 in 1980 (Laslett *et al*, 1998). Thus the use of non-inclusive arrangements grew dramatically in this period.

There were critics, though. A report by Her Majesty's Inspectors of Schools in 1974 suggested:

> Far too many children who may be described as socially maladjusted are being sent to boarding schools ... simply because they have shown behaviour which is a perfectly normal reaction to intolerable home conditions. (HMSO 1974 cited in Laslett *et al*, 1998)

The current youth justice system has parallels with some of the approaches described above, although the balance has shifted away from removal and exclusion. The current system includes options such as detention and training orders, or sentences spent in the community (section 90/91). There are options for part-time exclusion such as curfew orders and options for additional supervision such as local child curfews, supervision orders, community rehabilitation orders (including tagging), action plan orders and referral orders. There are also new options which include contracts with the individual concerned related to acceptable behaviour contracts and anti-social behaviour orders. Finally, there still exist reparation methods such as fines or reparation orders. (source: www.yjb.gov.uk/en-gb/yjs/SentencesOrdersand Agreements/accessed 10/1/07)

This brief historical overview reminds us that exclusion is not a new phenomenon. It is seen at societal and institutional levels. The way in which society deals with difference, particularly differences that manifest themselves in difficult or challenging behaviour, can be seen as a reflection of the view that society holds about its most vulnerable members. However, there are gaps between rhetoric and reality. The present educational climate in the UK which emphasises inclusion of all pupils nevertheless continues to operate a state sanctioned system that allows for pupils to be excluded from school.

In Part One of this book we offer the 'psychological perspectives' on exclusion that make up the first part of our book's title. We describe ways of viewing exclusion from two quite different perspectives. Firstly we use chaos theory as a means of reframing behaviour problems and behaviour change. Secondly, the chapter by Mike Solomon gives a perspective about exclusion drawn from psychodynamic psychology. These chapters set the scene for the case examples that are presented and discussed in Part Two.

1

Stability, Instability and Children's Behaviour

The introductory chapter outlined a history of exclusion as a method of social control. This chapter explores the nature of the conditions and processes which have led to exclusion. It examines different approaches to managing those excluded and presents a new perspective which explores alternative ways of describing, analysing and responding to problem behaviour.

Perception

The perception of *disease* is a prerequisite for any possible change in behaviour which might assist (or be thought to assist) in aiding the survival of both the afflicted and the rest of the population. Visible signs of disorders that might have been considered a threat include sensory and physical impairments, but in ancient Greek times Hippocrates considered that different behaviour or *mental disorder* was simply another disease. In the animal kingdom the cure for a disease was to allow time for the immune system to work. For Hippocrates cures came in the form of rest, purposeful work and good company.

Other healers such as Celcus used medicines such as extracts of hellebore which has a strong purgative effect, although if it failed, he resorted to treatment by violent means such as blows, whippings and use of chains. For a diseased animal, the priority was to find a place away from the other members of the herd, which offered as much protection from predators as possible; so too for humans. In Ancient Greek times the term 'asylum' was used. It referred to a place of safety and security. Families would seek asylum with friends or kin if they were being persecuted. Slaves unfairly or cruelly treated could go to a temple where it was an inviolable or religious offence to remove an individual by force, although the large number of deities at that time meant that respect for this concept was limited to followers of the particular occupier of the particular temple.

Containment

Within the framework of disease control, containment is a key element. So too in human behaviour containment is a feature for those people perceived as different and posing a threat. Early cloisters were established for the blind and records show that in AD 370 the Bishop of Caesarea cloistered many types of disabled together. A few such institutions were allocated the 'asylum' label. Nicholas, bishop of Myra (now in Turkey) provided dowries for the poor and disabled. (He is remembered as Saint Nicholas or Santa Claus). He established an institution in Gheel in Belgium where disabled children were given work in the fields.

However, the emphasis was on containment rather than treatment or cure. If people were cured, the attribution was generally towards religious miracles. The church became the institution to address those with nervous conditions such as epilepsy. Miracles were sought and, no doubt, occasionally found. The purveyors of such miracles became immortalised through canonisation to sainthood. For example, Saint John of Beverley in Yorkshire blessed a dumb man who was then cured. He became the patron saint for the deaf. Saint Augustine forbad disabled people from participating in church ceremonies. If you were deaf and dumb, you were unable to express your sins, therefore the protection of the church was unavailable. *Disease* was curable by human efforts, but the work of the devil was not.

A consequence of this belief was an exclusion from the civil rights enjoyed by other citizens. The disabled could not inherit, sign contracts or make wills. Some were harshly treated. There is a record of four blind men in 1425 being kitted out in full armour and placed in a square with a hog. The one who successfully killed the hapless animal won a prize. For people who talked to themselves, their mutterings were attributed to discussions with the devil. Some were locked up in 'idiot's cages'. In London, Bedlam (founded in the thirteenth century and revived in the seventeenth) was a popular destination for well-to-do families on a Sunday afternoon. Those confined there were considered mad.

The black death cast a shadow across medieval Europe. As many as one third of the human population died. Attribution was towards God's displeasure. The devil was responsible. Those who survived, but were traumatised and behaved differently were at risk of being considered demoniacally possessed. Witch hunts grew, heretics were sought and brought to trial or inquisition. Anyone with any kind of diversity was in danger of being considered a heretic. Single women, the disabled and those who appeared different were all at risk. Calvin taught that the mentally retarded were possessed by Satan, Luther proclaimed that they had no soul and that the devil was father to the idiots. The mentally handicapped were 'filled with Satan'. It was acceptable for such children to be drowned in the river. Treatments were attempted in some places, but if they failed, attribution of satanic possession was the consequence. The outlook for the individual was not good.

Others may have been luckier. Venice was a port from which soldiers fighting crusade wars set out. They returned injured, mutilated and perhaps unstable. As early as 1182 an 'Ospedale' was established for lepers, the destitute and crusaders. They would be cared for, fed and housed (Arnold and Baldouf-Burdes, 2002). A second was established to treat syphilis, a third for orphans, beggars and the sick, with the fourth for unwanted babies. (It was not until 1739 that London had an equivalent institution when Thomas Coram established the Foundling Hospital) They were religious institutions, but with a philosophy we would recognise today as humanitarian. Those protected by these institutions were treated with kindness rather than scorn.

Treatment

Within the animal kingdom, it is probably only mankind that has developed any systematic approach to assisting the healing processes found in nature. The step beyond containment was treatment. Healing has been part of ancient human activity, but we can highlight some early initiatives which have led to modern approaches to helping people with diverse conditions.

Healers have long been a part of human history. The Romans were concerned for the welfare of the state. A need to protect property and people from those deemed sick drove their treatment of madness. However the afflicted were perceived as having rights too and were provided with Guardians. Not all the culture of the Romans was lost when the Empire declined. By 533 AD scholars had compiled a 50 volume text on the treatment of the disabled, including the insane. Insane fathers were not able to give or withhold consent to the marriage of their daughters. Parents of insane children could nominate alternative heirs and those deemed insane were prohibited from marriage. When invaders from north of the Alps arrived, the codes for the treatment of these groups were aligned and remained standard until the eighteenth century.

From the time of the ancient Greeks there existed an ancient order that the deaf and dumb could not reason and therefore inherit property. However in medieval Spain, initiatives to teach existed. A Benedictine monk, Ponce de Leon, instructed deaf sons of wealthy families. Many learned to speak and were able to confess their sins, furnishing admittance to the church. It is likely that he used a form of sign language found in the monasteries of the time and the inescapable conclusion was revolutionary – the deaf were capable of being taught, given the appropriate methods. Special Education was born in 1578 in Spain. This spread to England in the seventeenth century and John Wallis took a lead in teaching deaf people. He was professor of geometry at Oxford and produced a text book on English grammar for foreigners in 1653 in which he highlighted the importance of education for the deaf. His work extended to teaching a congenitally deaf 25 year old to talk and he demonstrated his success at the Royal Society in 1661. At around the same time Bulwer published a volume describing methods of teaching deaf people, but went further than Wallis in calling for 'an academy of the mute'. Special Education was being discussed in England, even if it was not to become a reality for another 70 years with Henry Baker's tuition of the deaf.

The roots of the education system for those segregated from others by virtue of behaviour are found later. Of particular note is the influence of psychoanalysis which led to applications with young people.

Therapeutic approaches and children

The first half of the twentieth century saw the development of new therapeutic ideas often drawn from psychoanalytic theory. These would be applied to children described as Maladjusted in later legislation (Education Act 1944, HMSO). Some of the names associated with these experiments are still quite well known such as A S Neill with his Summerhill School; others, such as William Hunt, Otto Shaw and Leila Rendel, rather less so.

Neill was an exponent of psychoanalysis and provided it through *Private Lessons* for his pupils (Neill 1962). His description of their function plays down the therapeutic label: 'P.L.s were really a re-education. Their object was to lop off all complexes resulting from morality and fear' (Neill, 1962, p53).

At the turn of the twentieth century William Hunt established the Wallingford Farm Training Colony for (mainly) adolescents caught up in the nineteenth century poor law system. The ethos was a 'warm, restful, non-provocative environment', although others described the physical conditions as 'crude and squalid' (Bridgeland, 1971). Unfortunately the treatment of the individuals often involved violence and aggression in spite of Hunt's humanitarian principles.

Leila Rendel was the granddaughter of Sir Alexander Rendel, an eminent Victorian radical. The first world war had left a large number of women unable to marry because of the death of so many men. Her work led to the evolution of the Caldecott Community, one of the first schools to be recognised by the Board of Education under Section 80 of the 1921 Education Act as an appropriate (or *approved*) school for children who had been excluded from normal schools. The project provided direction for committed women with strong social consciences. The community offered a home to children from infancy, where needed.

Otto Shaw was an ardent user of psychoanalysis. His Red Hill School in Kent (arising out of the Caldecott Community) was not for all. He described his entry requirements:

> We do not take children with intelligence quotients below one hundred and thirty for we are, after all, a grammar school and there is more than a strong tradition of adventurous learning which, unfortunately, would leave a child of ordinary intelligence gasping. (Shaw, 1965, p16)

He described his philosophy:

> It is fatally easy to treat a delinquent in such a way that the symptom is repressed, but the basic urge that caused the anti-social action remains and, smouldering, will find an alternative route to the surface, being denied the first expression that it sought. (Shaw, 1965, p12)

The school was successful with a report published in 1968 reporting on nearly all of the children who had attended the school since 1943:

Cured	242
Cured/improved	29
Improved	44
Improved/failures	6
Failures	40
Withdrawn prematurely	28
(Died subsequently	7)
(In Bridgeland, 1971)	

However, in the 1960s and 1970s a new educational movement emerged. At the time it was called *Integration* and roots can be traced to the human rights movements found at that time. Later, in the 1990s the term integration gave way to the concept of Inclusion.

Inclusion

The 1981 Education Act was a key piece of educational legislation that set the scene for future developments in inclusive education. It removed the requirement to allocate categories to children. Instead, the concept of *special educational need* was introduced alongside a philosophical shift, that of integration. Integration introduced the notion that children with special needs should be educated alongside their peers in conventional mainstream schools. The subtle shift in terminology was to suggest that the child with special needs did not have to fit in with the majority, but that the educational systems needed to be adapted to include all children.

The economic recession in the early 1990s led to increased pressures on public service budgets. Residential schools and homes, fashionable in the early part of the century, were seen as expensive. Alternatives were sought, usually involving maintaining troubled and troublesome children in their own communities. This often created conflict within different local authority departments. An education department under pressure to save money would argue that the provision of the residential component of a special school or community was not their concern, but the province of social services. The same budget pressures were found in social service departments who would question whether they should rescue a child from a situation essentially brought about by a mainstream school's unwillingness to adapt its teaching to meet the needs of a difficult child. The consequence was a decline in the number of schools making residential provision for difficult children. At a policy level, this was not difficult. The philosophy was to include children in their local communities and to support children in mainstream settings.

Education, however, was changing. Four new phenomena were to drive the management of schools. All four were based on the concept of applying market forces, including competition, to education. They were:

- the introduction of national tests for 7, 11 and 14 year olds in addition to GCSEs for 16 year olds
- the publication of league tables of the results of those tests
- the publication of inspection reports from the newly formed Office for Standards in Education (Ofsted)

14

■ increasing financial independence and autonomy for schools

Pressures were placed on schools to improve their rankings in the national tests. This led to a conflict of interest. One easy way to improve exam results was to select those children who were likely to be successful in the exams. Thus there was a pressure to select, but additionally, there was (and still is) a pressure to exclude those children who were perceived to be a threat to those likely to be successful.

Yet at the same time schools were encouraged to *include* children with special educational needs. Extended schools offering a whole range of services to communities are being developed and built in ambitious and expensive programmes. The emphasis is on *social inclusion*. However, exclusion from school remains as a significant feature for many children. To further our understanding of this we now introduce a new and different way of examining children's behaviours and the ways that adults respond to them.

Exclusion – insights from Chaos Theory

Today, attribution of threat is now rarely a result of disease. We know that blindness and deafness are not contagious, yet we still exclude by means of segregated provision.

Exclusion from school is most frequently a consequence of children's behaviour being unacceptable to others.

For those working in our educational system, it is quite common to hear adults experiencing problem behaviours with a child to say things like:

'He misbehaves *all the time*.'

'He hits people *for no reason*.'

'When I see him first thing in the morning I just know *we're in for a bad day*.'

'He seems to kick off at the *slightest thing*.'

These statements can be considered quite cynically and a visiting professional (whether a psychologist or support teacher) who can look at the child in a dispassionate way may find that s/he behaves appropriately *some* of the time. Additionally, the child may be seen to be resilient against some provocations *some* of the time. The subsequent discussion with the poor suffering teacher is usually unsatisfactory. The teacher is shown data that demonstrate the apparent error of the above statements. We suggest, however, that we are missing a vital element of these statements – in other words:

'He misbehaves *all* the time.' is better described, 'He can misbehave at *any* time.'

'He hits people for no reason.' could be 'I cannot see any reason why he hits.'

'..in for a bad day.' becomes ' I can see from the start that he is different from previous days and I don't know why.'

'..kick off at the slightest thing.' becomes 'sometimes he kicks off and sometimes he does not. I can't see why.'

The common feature of these is the *unpredictability* of the problem behaviour. In other words, the child's behaviour is *unstable*.

A theory of unstable systems

Our understanding of unstable systems in a wide range of areas has developed over the last 40 years with a dramatic increase in publicity over the last 20. The popular label is *Chaos Theory,* but there are other descriptions including *non-linear system theory,* or the *theory of complex systems.* The term chaos can lead to misunderstandings, though. Within this context it does not relate to random events, but events that are covered by a complex system of interconnecting rules.

Non-linear development will inevitably occur if we have the following conditions:

- the learning process is iterative. The output from one learning cycle acts as the input for the next
- at least three (but ideally many more) items are competing for the attention of the learner
- the learner's attention is a finite commodity – attending to (or learning) one thing means that less attention can be given to another
- there are no large scale, predetermined forces or architectures that determine what is learned

Demonstrations of non-linear development may include:

- sudden jumps and changes in children's learning and behaviour
- delayed effects of different kinds of teaching and experiences
- variation in uncertainty in the course of development. There will be times when learning and behaviour appear steady and almost linear and other times when they might appear almost random
- a limit to the extent you can predict future learning and behaviour. The term 'prediction horizon' has been used to describe this

- at each level of analysis more detail becomes visible
- there will be greater variability in behaviour before and after a sudden change in the child's situation. These 'chaotic markers' can signal that such a change is imminent.

If we apply this to difficult and challenging behaviour we may find non-linear development such as:

- children can change their behaviour quite quickly
- apparently insignificant events can become highly significant later on
- things can appear to be going well for a time, but can change quickly
- it's impossible to predict (anticipate) more than the immediate future
- there is never a full analysis – each level of explanation can be added to. You never have 'the full story'
- there are signals to be detected just before something big happens. Things take a little time to calm down following a big change

Sources of instability in children's behaviour

Some possible sources of instability in children's behaviour include are suggested in Table 1.1.

Death of parent
Unstable housing
Separation of parents
Illness or injury
Change in health of member of family
New family members (reconstituted families)
Birth of a sibling
Arguments between parents
Family member leaves home
Change in schools
Change in routines eg SATS, festivals, Christmas
Change in class/friendships

Table 1.1 Examples of sources of instability for children

Many of these items are found in a well known list for adults – the social readjustment rating scale used to model environmental risk factors for heart attacks. The numbers indicate the relative strength of the factor.

Factor	Weighting
Death of spouse	100
Divorce	73
Marital Separation	65
Jail Term	63
Death of close family member	63
Personal injury or illness	53
Marriage	50
Fired at work	47
Marital Reconciliation	45
Retirement	45
Change in health of family member	44
Pregnancy	40
Sexual difficulties	39
Gain of new family member	39
Business readjustment	39
Change in financial state	38
Death of close friend	37
Change of different line of work	36
Change in number of arguments with spouse	35
Large mortgage	31
Foreclosure of mortgage or loan	30
Change in responsibilities at work	29
Son or daughter leaving home	29
Trouble with in-laws	29
Outstanding personal achievement	28
Spouse begins or stops work	26
Beginning or ending school	26
Change in living conditions	25
Revision of personal habits	24
Trouble with boss	23
Change in work hours or conditions	20
Change in residence	20
Change in school	20
Change in recreation	19
Change in church activities	19
Change in social activities	18
Middle size mortgage	17
Change in sleeping habits	16
Change in number of family get togethers	15
Change in eating habits	15
Holidays	13
Christmas	12
Minor violations of the law	11

Table 1.2 Social Readjustment rating scale, Holmes and Rahe, 1967

There is evidence for a link between instability and children being per-manently excluded from secondary schools. A study in a UK city revealed the following risk factors in 31 children who had been permanently excluded. The numbers indicate how often each risk factors was found in the sample:

Mental Health Problems	8
Special Educational Needs (SEN)	14
Looked After Children (LAC)	1
Single parent	11
Disabled parent	5
Domestic violence	8
Parental rejection	14
Parental substance misuse	4
Parental mental health	4
Parental reports of behaviour management problems	18
Child Protection Register	8
No fixed abode/rough sleeping	4
Risk of sexual exploitation	3

Table 1.3 Risk factors for permanent exclusion (Pitchford, M, 2006 personal communication)

There is considerable support for these in the literature, for example Grim-shaw (1994). We can extend our enquiry to include young people who are older than the statutory school leaving age.

NEET risk factors

Young people can be excluded from more institutions than just school. A new category of young people has drawn interest recently. This refers to those not in employment, education or training (NEET). Young people who fall within this category are likely to experience social exclusion. The opportunities for engaging in economic activity are greatly reduced for the vast majority of this group. Recent work identifying risk factors in the West Midlands suggests that young people are more likely to end up in this group include:

Unstable accommodation	Involvement with the Youth Offending Team
Low motivation (no idea of what to do after statutory school leaving)	School attendance < 80%
A history of poor behaviour in school	Categorised as having a Learning Difficulty or Disability (LDD)
Unemployment in family	
Poor basic skills	

Table 1.4: Risk Factors for NEET status at age 17. (Arnold, 2009)

Note the similarities of the lists. The common features have instability in different domains of people's lives. The concept of NEET is relatively new for psychologists and one which we shall not elaborate here. However, the raising of the school leaving age and increase in interest in helping young people into the world of work is likely to focus more attention on this vulnerable group.

Mental Health Risk Factors

An important element in exclusion is found in those with mental health difficulties. For the sake of completeness we briefly consider mental health risk factors. The National Children's Home (NCH) has a definition of risk factors: 'any factor or combination of factors that increases the chance of an undesirable outcome affecting a person' (NCH, 2007). Such factors can be categorised:

Within child:	Within family:	Within community:
Specific learning difficulties	Overt parental conflict	Socio-economic
Communication difficulties	Family breakdown	disadvantage
Specific developmental	Inconsistent or unclear	Homelessness
delay	discipline	Disaster
Genetic influence	Hostile or rejecting	Discrimination
Difficult temperament	relationships	Other significant life events
Physical illness especially	Failure to adapt to child's	
if chronic and/or	changing needs	
neurological	Physical, sexual or	
Academic failure	emotional abuse	
Low self-esteem	Parent psychiatric illness	
	Parental criminality,	
	alcoholism or personality	
	disorder	
	Death and loss – including	
	loss of friendship	

Table 1.5 Mental Health Risk Factors NCH (2007)

If we examine the within family and within community lists we find similarity to other lists cited above. A common element is lack of stability. Instability causes stress and can lead to health (including mental health) difficulties. Instability can lead to exclusion.

Instability within school

It is possible actually to *increase* the instability for children by some current educational practices perhaps designed to help children with difficulties.

Consider the following sequence that is common for children who are beginning to show signs of troublesome behaviour:

Teacher:	Pupils:
First reaction: Do nothing – hope problem will sort itself out using usual systems.	First reaction: I understand the system and I choose to behave badly. It's not my fault anyway.
Second reaction: Begin to worry or get anxious. This problem isn't going to go away. Communicate anxiety non-verbally.	Second reaction: More of same, but I sense something is changing.
Third reaction: Do something radical – call parent and/or outside agency.	Third reaction: The system has suddenly changed – greater instability.
Fourth outcome: Write individual behaviour programme.	Fourth reaction: Need to adjust to new rules, greater instability.

Table 1.6 Sequences in teacher and pupil behaviour

For children there are sources of instability that may be associated with introducing an *Individual Behaviour Programme* (IBP):

- sudden change in amount of adult attention
- being no longer seen as part of the crowd
- having no reference group or experience of implications
- sudden increase in number of adults involved
- each adult may have different ideas about what their role is. From the child's perspective there is confusion about different expectations with different adults

Each of these elements is likely actually to increase instability for the child and our thesis is that instability leads to exclusion. Additionally there are processes outside school which also contribute to instability. We wish to highlight two phenomena – the *Agency Game* and *Pass the Parcel.*

The Agency Game

We use the term 'games' in this context to describe actions undertaken by individuals and groups which have similarities of structure and function, but involve a set of rules and assumptions which may not be clear to a third party. We will begin with a game played by clients and families – the Agency Game.

If a parent or family has a problem that is complex, they may seek assistance from an external agency. There are many to choose from:

- family doctors
- schools
- education or children's services
- social workers
- educational welfare officers
- educational psychologists
- parental partnership services
- solicitors
- housing officers
- school nurse

The range of problems reported is great. It includes children misbehaving at school, misbehaving at home, not wanting to go to school, reporting bullying, wetting the bed, not thriving, not eating, not learning to read/do other curriculum related things, who are always active or who communicate in odd ways. This list is not exhaustive.

The person worried about the issue may present it to the external agency which may offer an opinion or advice to the enquirer. However the outcome of the enquiry or referral may not be what the enquirer expected or wanted to hear. This can be a source of *cognitive dissonance*, causing some distress and confusion. Cognitive dissonance describes the psychological discomfort arising from an individual finding two opposing pieces of knowledge at the same time (Festinger, 1957). In this case the enquirer may hold a belief about the nature of the problem (for example there is something wrong with the child), but find that the agency suggests a different account (the parent's management of the child needs to change). One possible resolution to that dissonance, distress and confusion is for the individual to approach a different agency in the hope that they might obtain a more acceptable response. It is likely that the enquirer will receive many different explanations or perspectives from the agencies they consult. The consumer of the service is more likely to attend to the opinion that is perceived to favour their case.

The single explanation or perspective is not to be found in these circumstances.

A particularly acute example of this occurred after a BBC documentary on the condition Attention Deficit/Hyperactivity Disorder (ADHD) in 1995.

A parent watching the documentary noticed similarities between the children described on television and her own son. She went to her GP and described the situation. The GP completed the appropriate checklist, agreed that there was a high probability that the child met the criteria for ADHD and prescribed medication. Unknown to the GP, the family were also involved with Social Services. When the parent updated the social worker with the diagnosis, the social worker realised that the family might be entitled to attendance allowance (now called the Disabled Living Allowance), as ADHD was a recognised medical condition that required supervision. Their application was successful and the family were given weekly payments.

When other families in the area found out that this family had obtained an attendance allowance after describing problematic behaviour to their GP, more went to their GPs, described their children in the same way and were given the medication. The incidence of prescribing this medication dramatically increased in this area. However, one GP was uneasy about this and wanted additional corroborative evidence rather than simply the descriptions from the parents. The parent's response was to ask for a change of GP to one who would agree to the medication (and subsequent payments). (It is said, but there is no evidence, that the parents did not risk giving their children the medication, but sold it on the black market as a barbiturate. Thus a situation had arisen in which the State was inadvertently sponsoring drug dealing.)

At each point, the participants in the above situation were acting rationally. No one can be blamed for their actions. It was resolved by the prescription of this particular medication being centralised. However, the point is sharply made. If citizens are *consumers* (or *users*) of services and choice is encouraged, parents and families will make choices that produce more favourable outcomes in their eyes. Hence the agency game is a logical one for the participants to play.

Pass the Parcel

The second game is played by the professionals.

When presented with a complex situation, agencies such as social services, health and children's services may ask a number of questions to establish both entitlement to services and appropriateness of services. Such questions routinely include information about what the client (or prospective client) has done already and what other agencies have offered. Depending on the answers to the questions, the agency may determine whether they should offer assistance.

On the face of it, this seems reasonable enough, but in practice it is much more complex and problematic. Consider the following situation. This is based on many real cases.

A 12 year old boy is behaving badly at school. There has been a deterioration in that child's behaviour over the last few months. The parents are invited in to discuss the situation. The parent who attends discloses that her partner has just left the family and they are at risk of losing the house. The neighbours are complaining of the bad behaviour of the 12 year old in the area. The parent and the school generate an idea that the child is not coping well with the departure of the other parent. An agreed outcome is that the child should be offered counselling through the health services. The parent goes to the GP and asks for a referral to a counselling service. The parent and child are given an appointment. The child does not want to go and possibly responds by saying 'I ain't going to no psycho – I ain't a nutter', but the parent persuades the child to go. The questions are asked. What brings you here? Discussion about the child's behaviour in school arises. The parent and the counsellor generate an idea that this needs to be managed through a behaviour pro-gramme in school, as this is one area causing great concern. The counselling service offers follow up, but the child is adamant that they are not going and the family fail to attend follow up sessions. The counselling service closes the case.

The school is left with a troubled and troublesome child. The school sees the causes as being within the family (this family are not coping). The family see the causes as within the child (he's not coping with the departure of the parent). The counselling service sees the problem as within the school (a school based behaviour management programme is needed).

Cognitive dissonance may well be a feature for the professional here too. Many services have limited resources and have to prioritise services given to clients. The question of 'whose problem it is and who should be assisting' is easier to resolve by framing it as somebody else's issue rather than admitting that you or your service is failing the child. Each agency is acting rationally, but framing the hypotheses as within somebody else's domain. This is the feature that defines 'pass the parcel'. These two games are frequently both features of and contributors to the instability of the situations surrounding children who end up excluded from school.

We now turn to a phenomenon well described in the psychological literature.

Attribution

Instability can arise from the absence of a large scale scheme or plan. Whilst it might be tempting to look for global laws or rules describing our educational systems (Curriculum, SATS, GSCEs, etc) at an individual level these may be less influential than more local events. The descriptions we use for negative events may be more influenced by the person describing the event than often thought. Ross (1977) coined the term *fundamental attribution error* to describe the tendency for subjects to attribute the same behaviour to situational factors whereas observers attribute behaviour to dispositional features of the person observed. In other words, if I am asked to explain why something I did went wrong, I am more likely to attribute the actions externally, that is I may blame something other than myself. However people observing me are more likely to blame me and attribute the error to something within me rather than the external factor that I considered. This leads to a situation where explanations are different and dependent on different observers. So any perception of the 'problem' is likely to be dependent on the perspective of the person describing it, not some external and independent agent. The existence of these multiple explanations and perspectives makes one large-scale explanation very difficult to create. When Van Geert (1994) describes the large-scale plans, forces or architecture this would imply one overriding perspective or explanation. This is rarely found.

For example:

A child behaves in some way deemed unacceptable. The child will say, 'it wasn't my fault, it was X who started it.' The adult watching the event is more likely to attribute the behaviour to some feature of the child. Bringing in more stakeholders adds to the possible different attributions. Consider the following participants:

- the child
- the child's family
- the excluding school
- the receiving school/unit

It is quite acceptable for schools to attribute children's poor behaviour to the family. Families often attribute difficulties in school to poor teaching. The theories used by each group can lead to differences in approach, often with confusing outcomes for the children concerned. Children attribute their behaviour to other children or to the teachers. Teachers in units attribute behaviour to children's previous experiences rather than elements in their own units. For example, a unit based on psychotherapeutic lines may advocate children being empowered to express themselves in many different ways, whilst a large school may be run along lines regulated by rules, rewards and sanctions. One possible explanation for the child's behaviour in the excluding school might be to attribute it to a dysfunctional family, whilst the family attributes it to teachers who can't control children. The family may believe that the teachers need to change and the teachers believe that the family needs to change.

Types of change

When educational programmes are introduced there is an implicit assumption that they will effect change for the child. Additionally, there is usually an expectation that the change will be gradual and linear. In other words, the child's behaviour will slowly but surely improve. Unfortunately this is not usually the case for change in non-linear systems. As a general rule, the change itself will be non-linear.

Linear change is characterised by the direction of change remaining more or less constant. If we take a medical drug, we do not expect to feel completely better straight away, but we do expect to feel increasingly better over time. If the drug made us feel worse, we would question its use. Other examples of linear change are found in most pieces of technical equipment. If we turn the volume control clockwise on a radio, we expect the sound output to increase. A small turn creates a small change and a larger turn creates a larger change. We would question the workings of the the volume control if a small turn of the knob created a large increase, but a further turning led to a reduction of the sound. We expect linearity in these circumstances. We could visualise this as:

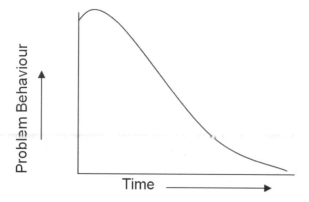

Figure 1.1: Linear change

We might accept some variation from this, but the underlying trend should more or less follow the line.

Non-linear change does not follow that pattern. There will be gains and losses, periods of great change and some of none. Worse, there will be regression and times when the programme is doubted, simply because of the presence of non-linearities. We can visualise these changes as:

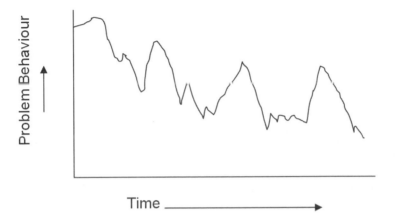

Figure 1.2: Non-linear change

Unstable systems usually change in non-linear ways.

Stages of Change

Van Geert (1994) has identified three stages following change in unstable systems. These can be applied to the introduction of an IBP as follows:

1. Interest contagion (honeymoon). There is enthusiasm for the IBP. The pupil finds lots of opportunities to earn rewards. He/she tries really hard.

2. Saturation (boredom). Novelty begins to wear off. The pupil becomes rather used to rewards and even bored by them.

3. Recovery (regression). The pupil begins to ignore the programme and return to old habits. The pupil tests the system. Is this new system consistent for the pupil?

We can illustrate this graphically:

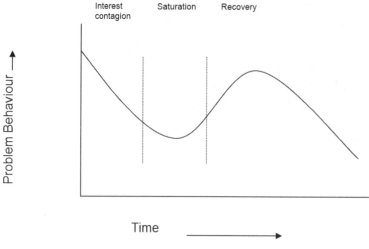

Figure 1.3: Van Geert's Cycle

The problems these different stages create for teaching staff who are expecting linear change are clear. If the expectation is that the child improves incrementally day after day and this does not occur, the obvious conclusion to draw is that the programme is not working. In fact, it is probably the case that evidence that the programme is working can only be recognised after at least one complete cycle of contagion/saturation and recovery. However, the temptation is to abandon the programme in favour of the previous status quo. After all, the behaviour might actually be worse than it was prior to the introduction of the programme.

We can demonstrate some of these elements by looking at data from a practical application of these methods of analysis.

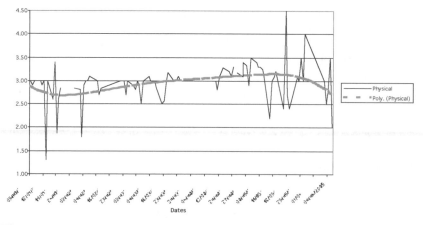

Figure 1.4: Example of behaviour chart.

28

The chart plots points earned each day by a child on a behaviour programme in a pupil referral unit (PRU). The smoother line is created by an analysis of the daily points score and shows overall trends over time. The higher the line, the more points were earned, reflecting better behaviour. Shortly after the programme was introduced, the pupil challenged the system with the resulting large variation in day-to-day performance. It took some time before the programme began to show positive benefits. The instability is evident and near the end of the illustration the degree of instability increased dramatically. In this case it reflected the child's mother giving birth to a new baby. The variation in the behaviour is quite apparent. The behaviour becomes more unstable.

Conclusions

Instability is a significant factor which can lead to children being excluded from school. The complexity of factors affecting children excluded from school leads to instability in many areas of their lives. One feature leading to instability is the lack of an overarching plan or single perspective. Interventions by professionals can lead to greater (not lesser) instability for children.

Schools are being encouraged to meet a wide range of needs of local communities. However, schools which are not appearing to raise the level of attainment of their pupils (as measured by exam results) are heavily criticised by the current inspection framework.

The pressures to create a stable set of indicators showing school performance can create situations which are not conducive to working with very unstable children.

2

A Psychodynamic Perspective

Mike Solomon

An alternative title for this chapter might be: **Trying to understand the ins and outs: Reflections on the systems psychodynamics of school exclusion**.

As a Clinical Psychologist working in two places – a Child and Adolescent Mental Health (CAMH) clinic and a Pupil Referral Unit (PRU) for excluded school children – I move in and out of two complex organisations. Working as a mental health professional within education, I continually find myself facing questions such as: Where do I belong? Am I inside or outside? Which system am I a part of? Where do I want to be?

Parallels might be drawn with the experience of children excluded from mainstream school, together with their parents, carers and families, who have to move between mainstream and specialist education providers. They too may be uncertain about their place in the education system, and are likely to have thoughts about where they would like to be placed, or place themselves.

The factors involved in exclusion from school are complex. While the apparent reasons behind school exclusion may be all too obvious, this chapter attempts to outline some of the less obvious influences and pressures that lie behind the wish to exclude certain children from our schools.

I introduce the ideas of systems and tasks, relate them to education, and then outline some of the unconscious dynamics that underlie exclusion. These processes can help us understand some of the pressures to exclude from mainstream schools, and to keep excluded, some of the most vulnerable and troubled children and young people in our society. The complex interactions between these pupils, their families, and the schools, education and wider systems they encounter are considered, with emphasis on what may be underlying these relationships. Some implications for policy, practice and provision are then drawn out.

Systems and Tasks

A system can be defined as a set of activities that take place within a boundary that transform something (an input) into something different (an output) (Miller and Rice, 1967; Roberts, 1994). The concept began in biology, where living creatures can be thought of as open systems. If a system becomes closed, with either no new inputs or outputs, then it will perish. In organisational terms, a system requires its boundaries to be managed if it is to remain open. Any organisation that becomes a closed system will not survive.

In educational terms, a school can be thought of as an open system, in which new inputs (children) are transformed into different outputs (more educated children). The idea of schools as systems is not new (eg Bazalgette, 1989; Obholzer, 1996; Sutoris, 2000), and while the question of the task(s) assigned to education systems by society is a complex one, it is interesting to consider the question of the task of education in relation to pupils who are on the margins of the mainstream.

There are different ways of thinking about the task of a system or organisation (Lawrence, 1977; Roberts, 1994). The normative task is the formal or official task which the organisation is supposed to be carrying out. This may be contained within the mission statement or literature of the organisation, which everyone involved can refer to. The existential task is that which people involved think they are carrying out, – what they believe they are really here to do. The phenomenological task is what it looks like people are doing – the task that can be inferred from people's behaviour as if perceived by an outside observer, and of which they themselves may not be consciously aware.

So what may be the task(s) of education systems with respect to those pupils on the margins of mainstream? We can think of the normative task in terms of the promotion and prioritisation of rehabilitation, reintegration and inclusion, bringing with it the possibility of change and transformation. This relies on exclusion settings being established and maintained as open systems. Paul Cooper (2004) places the emphasis on social and academic engagement, with the choice of provision dependent on its ability to provide opportunities and support for this aim. This depends on professional autonomy and flexibility of provision (Cooper, 2005) if this shared societal task is to be achieved. This is the challenge faced by policy-makers (most recently, at the time of writing, the UK Government's White Paper *Back on Track*, DCSF, 2008).

However, in practice there may be evidence of another aspect of the task of education systems in relation to vulnerable and challenging pupils. There are likely to be desires within mainstream schools for excessively disruptive, troubling and troubled pupils to be removed, regardless of the quality and appropriateness of any alternative provision. These wishes may be experienced consciously in terms of the existential task (what we think we're doing) or unconsciously acted out as if carrying out a phenomenological task available to observation (what others may see us doing).

Such a phenomenological task may be based on unconscious desires to remove challenging pupils into exclusion settings that can act as closed systems, and for these pupils never to return. In society generally, there is a wish – not necessarily conscious – for school exclusion to be managed by the use of closed systems. Wishes to 'lock 'em out' or 'lock 'em up' are very strong, with the urge that certain children be sent away, never to return. Such wishes apply not only to children excluded from school, as there are other examples from our exclusive and excluding society. Recent history illustrates society's reaction to people with learning disabilities and those with significant mental health problems, by building large institutions with locked doors. The recurring debate about prison ships as a political and practical solution to the growing prison population in the UK seems to embody the unconscious phantasy that such vessels will not remain anchored and can be cast adrift, never to return. Further back in history, one might even view the establishment of Australia as a penal colony on the opposite side of the world to the UK as another way of fulfilling such wishes.

Conscious and unconscious reasons for exclusion

The apparent reasons why children are excluded from school are all too obvious. According to the UK Government's Department for Children, Schools and Families (DCSF) website, the major categories of explanation given include disruptive behaviour, physical assault, threatening behaviour and verbal abuse. Other reasons include drugs and alcohol, damage to property, theft and bullying.

However, I argue that there are other, less obvious but very powerful influences and pressures that lie behind school exclusion. To support this argument, I draw on ideas from psychoanalytic, systemic and group analytic perspectives. The understanding offered by these approaches includes the tendency towards unconscious splitting and projection (Klein, 1946), the wish to evacuate and get rid of what we find uncomfortable and the creation of what Paul Hoggett (2000) calls 'The Other' that makes it easier to do this. In addition, there are ways to think about how the excluded both position themselves and are positioned in society (Davies and Harre, 1990), as well as the societal response to such positioning (Scanlon and Adlam, in press). I will now try to outline each of these in turn.

Splitting and projection

According to a psychoanalytic view of development, it takes time and repeatedly good enough experience for an infant to begin to experience the world in an integrated way. Initially, experiences are fragmented, and uncomfortable feelings can be difficult to tolerate. It can be difficult to tolerate both good and bad, and difficult or bad feelings can be disowned and projected outside, elsewhere, onto or into someone else. Infants' cries are an excellent way of doing this, making any responsive adult carer concerned, anxious and uncomfortable, and moved to take action to alleviate the baby's discomfort and unease. The infant's thoughts, feelings and experience are fragmented and disintegrated, and there is a need for another to contain these fragmented anxieties in order for the infant to feel held. Such containment can be offered by responding to discomfort through action, but also through putting thoughts and feelings into words (Bion, 1962, 1967). If good enough containment is offered and experienced repeatedly, then the infant can begin to feel understood. This offers the possibility of being understood again. This notion of containment is very different to its colloquial usage, where containment is something concrete to hold in place physically something (or someone) troublesome.

In adulthood too, we can all move between more and less integrated emotional and mental states (Klein, 1959). When our anxieties are not contained sufficiently, we can be unable to tolerate our thoughts, feelings and anxieties, and so may split them off, and project them elsewhere. In Kleinian language, this state of mind is referred to as the 'paranoid-schizoid position' (Klein, 1946). Emotional development can be thought of in terms of movement towards the so-called depressive position (not the same as depressed), in which anxieties and difficult thoughts and feelings may be tolerated, and in which there is a capacity to think about them in a more integrated way. As adults we move between these two positions all the time.

Just like individuals, we can think of systems and organisations being more and less able to tolerate anxieties, and moving between paranoid-schizoid and depressive position functioning. Effective management and decision-making need, among other things, time, the capacity to tolerate uncertainty, curiosity and a wish to understand, as well as a capacity to keep thinking under pressure. When organisations are not able to offer these conditions, decisions can be made reactively, with less thought or understanding, and the organisation itself can be experienced as functioning in a paranoid-schizoid way. The pressures to act, and to re-act, may mean that the space for understanding that is essential for containment (Winnicott, 1971) is squeezed out, leaving less opportunity for depressive position thinking.

Evacuation

The individual model of unconscious splitting and projection can also be applied to groups and societies as a whole. On a societal level, certain groups may be used as targets for projections when paranoid-schizoid functioning predominates. Bad feelings may be got rid of by getting rid of the people and groups who are identified as carrying such feelings. This is one way of thinking about prejudice of any kind in society. One way of thinking about the outcome of these processes is the creation of 'The Other', defined by Paul Hoggett as 'a container for that which I cannot bear' (2000, p60). The creation of this 'Other' offers us the illusion of comfort when it is made invisible. There is a wish to make excluded, or exclude-able, groups invisible to mainstream society, so that out of sight is out of mind. In the story of Oedipus, the citizens of Thebes both know and don't want to know his plight, and so they turn a blind eye to his situation. So too in our society there is a shared wish to turn a blind eye to the plight of vulnerable groups (Steiner, 1985). Historically, children out of school, adults in mental hospitals and long-stay institutions have all been rendered invisible to mainstream society. While provision for children out of school, and excluded from school, has developed significantly over time, I argue that they still operate in the context of these unconscious societal desires that strive to make such groups of children and young people invisible to the mainstream.

Impact on staff

In this context, unconscious societal pressures must have an impact on the professionals who work with groups of excluded children. Staff themselves can become identified with excluded groups, and, like their pupils, risk becoming invisible to the mainstream. Staff groups in exclusion zones may themselves come to feel separate and segregated. This leaves such staff caught in a dilemma, as to whether to feel devalued and ignored by 'the main-stream', or to speak out and risk being seen as troublesome and challenging (again, just like the excluded children themselves).

If staff feel segregated and cut off, there is likely to be a clear impact on their work with excluded pupils. History shows us that closed systems, and the mentality of staff teams who feel invisible to the outside world, have tended to breed unprofessional and occasionally abusive practice. The more that staff in institutions are out of touch with colleagues elsewhere, the less em-phasis there is likely to be on professional development and training, profes-sional accountability and overall quality. The consequences for people they work with can be serious.

Impact on policy

These unconscious pressures can also feed into the formulation of education and social policy. An extreme illustration of this came in the UK in 1993, after the murder of toddler Jamie Bulger by two ten year old boys. This was a shocking event, and its implications were very hard to tolerate and face, parti-cularly the questions it raised for the society in which such a thing could happen. The political wish for splitting and projection was evident in the words of the Prime Minister, John Major, when he responded by saying 'It is time to understand a little less, and condemn a little more'. There followed statements about a 'crusade against crime' that advocated the setting up of 'secure training centres to detain persistent 12-15 year old offenders'. Such a move can be seen as an enactment of the wish to 'lock 'em up' and to manage the evacuation of distress and disturbance through splitting and projection and establishing a closed system. All disturbance, upset, vulnerability and de-linquency was located in a small group of young people, with little or no capacity to think about those features being part of society generally. The fervour called upon in a 'crusade' emphasised the lack of space for curiosity, understanding or thinking.

Positioning in relation to the mainstream

One way of thinking about what happens in the relationship between the excluded and those who exclude, is by using the concept of positioning (Davies and Harre, 1990).

Positions in society are not simply static roles, but emerge dynamically through interactions. We all have opportunities to adopt positions and we may assign positions to others. Positions are continually offered, accepted or resisted through interactions and negotiations. This is a helpful idea in considering the possibility of pupils and families making choices to take up positions of being outside mainstream education. They may not simply be at the mercy of powerful decision-makers such as head teachers, governors and local authorities, but also have agency and power themselves in taking up positions in relation to education.

There are a number of reasons why families might take up a position of refusing to feel that accommodation in the mainstream is appropriate or desirable. Background family factors for excluded children include: early separation from primary carer; bereavement; serious parental illness; mental illness in the family; and substance misuse and/or criminality in the family. It is very common for there to be multiple factors involved (Rendall and Stuart, 2005). In my experience, such factors are often combined with other background circumstances including: domestic violence; abuse and neglect; children in public care; families who are refugees from conflict and war zones; dislocation, displacement and trauma; and inter-generational patterns of behaviours and relationships.

But as we consider the interactions and relationships between such families and our education systems, can we also examine ourselves, and the mainstream society we find ourselves in as professionals? When I was working with Dwayne, a 13 year old pupil in the PRU, he asked me 'Why is it called 'mainstream'?' I replied that I wasn't quite sure, and that it was a very interesting question. I then responded by going to the dictionary. Mainstream is defined as the principal, dominant, widely accepted group. It is also a river having tributaries – the main stream – that by definition is an open system, as it has inputs flowing into it and integration in its essence. There is also the verb, to mainstream, meaning to join or be placed in the mainstream.

We might examine our own reactions to being viewed as part of a principal, dominant, widely accepted group. We can all think of ourselves like Groucho Marx (1959) when he said 'I don't care to belong to a club that accepts people like me as members'. For excluded children and families, there are many reasons why mainstream schools may not feel safe or appropriate for their needs. Pupils and families may position themselves outside 'mainstream' in order to feel safe, more contained, better able to function, more integrated and less lost. Parents sometimes tell my colleagues and myself that they are happy that their child has been placed in the PRU, as they think that smaller classes, higher staffing ratios and more attention will meet their child's needs better. These are all part of helping to make such children and families feel more safe and secure. Such containment – in the psychoanalytic and psychological sense – offered through understanding and the management of open systems, is very different to the concrete containment and closed systems that may unconsciously be wished for in parts of society.

Positioning and mirroring

In the relationship between the excluded and mainstream society and education, it is essential to reflect on what happens when particular pupils and/or their families refuse to be included. Society (and its representatives – schools and education services) may respond by mirroring. This happens when one party in an interaction retaliates by copying, mimicking and reproducing the actions of the other party. This usually involves instant reaction, without much thought and processing about the possible meanings of the initial action. There is a lack of containment and thinking, and the interaction consists solely of action and reaction. This way of being is common in the lives of pupils and families who position themselves outside mainstream education. Refusal to attend, behave or learn according to mainstream expectations tends to provoke reaction. Schools and education services, as well as other societal agencies, are not immune from mirroring such refusal. The societal reaction might in turn involve refusing, including taking action to exclude a child from mainstream school. The challenge facing mainstream schools and services is that it is very hard to know how to relate to the refusal of the child or family.

One way that makes it difficult to know how to relate or respond to the child and/or family is the view of intentionality held by the mainstream. Often this view is that, by virtue of their behaviour, the pupil is seen as intentionally choosing to be outside norms, which in turn exerts a pull towards a reaction by exclusion. The challenge is, therefore, how to deliver normative education to those who stand outside such norms.

The challenge of reintegration

So how might mainstream schools and services respond to the refusal of the child or family? Without sufficient containment and space for thinking (Winnicott, 1971), there may not be a wish or a capacity to understand. There is only a wish to react, and to act upon the unconscious desires outlined above. A desire to exclude may override other considerations, and make it hard or impossible to think about the needs of the pupil and what may be an appropriate alternative placement to meet those needs.

Exclusion may not be the only reaction to these pupils and families. The idea of reintegration itself can also become a reaction, whereby there is a wish to place the excluded pupil back into a different mainstream school as soon as possible, for their reintegration. However, this is not always the most appropriate or helpful response. The question of appropriate placement is crucial (Cooper, 2004), and relies on the capacity to contain, think about and understand pupils' and families' needs, anxieties and preoccupations. There also needs to be an assessment of the extent to which exclusion is the outcome of the pupil's or family's refusal, or of the mainstream school system's response. This all needs careful assessment – of and with the child, family and school system.

While reintegration is often thought about in terms of school systems, another way to conceptualise it is in terms of psychological reintegration. We all feel more together when we feel our anxieties are contained and understood, when we feel safe and secure. This is certainly the case for pupils and families who have refused mainstream education, at least temporarily. This means that the task of 'reintegration' is to understand how best to promote the psychic re-integration of the excluded pupil and their family, and to consider what an appropriate educational placement would be, as part of an intervention plan.

Understanding and hope

Pupil Referral Units (or whatever they will be called following the UK Government's White Paper, *Back on Track*, DCSF, 2008) can play a key role in providing a focus for trying to understand what lies behind a school exclusion. One key success criterion for PRUs is the degree to which staff offer pupils the possibility of a second chance or fresh start (Ofsted, 2007). Such a possibility needs to be based on attempts at explicit understanding and appropriate placement.

In my experience in a Pupil Referral Unit it is all too clear where a pupil is being referred from, and where referred to, at the time of exclusion. However, the question of what a pupil might be being referred *for*, is rarely, if ever, asked. The role of PRUs can be to offer assessment and the possibility of understanding. PRUs have the potential to be experienced as a 'secure base' (Bowlby, 1982) by pupils and families. PRUs can be experienced as predictable, safe and secure environments providing clear boundaries and caring, thoughtful and understanding relationships and support. They can help pupils and families to feel more integrated and held, giving them the experience of being inside somewhere. PRUs can be experienced as containing, open systems, and can make key contributions to placing pupils appropriately, promoting psychic integration wherever pupils are placed.

Example

Paul was a 13 year old boy who was permanently excluded for having a knife in school. He had previously been involved in fighting and bullying. He had previously been placed on the child protection register for neglect. Through the multi-disciplinary assessment in the PRU it emerged that he lacked confidence and social skills, and chose to side with 'bullies' to avoid becoming a 'victim' himself. Intensive interventions with him in and out of class, together with therapeutic work with him individually and with his family, helped to support him and his parents. Paul's family became more able to manage and sustain the changes they had begun, and Paul was able to manage being placed in a different mainstream school. Ongoing support was offered to him, his family and the school, and he was able to remain at school and succeed academically and socially.

Implications for policy

Exclusion is complicated. Answers and solutions to issues of exclusion and reintegration are not easily or readily available. Indeed, it is the capacity to tolerate and even embrace complexity that is crucial to finding effective ways to make a positive impact on the lives of excluded young people.

Societal pressure towards managing exclusion using closed systems can be seen as a defensive response to anxieties about pain, grief, chaos and out-of-control feelings. The inherent risk within open systems is reacting in turn to the pressure for this reaction – either by 'including at all costs' or by fighting with the mainstream. So both exclusion and reactive reintegration can be thought of as responses to anxiety. The challenge to find space, time and ways to understand and think about the needs of challenging and vulnerable pupils and their families is to establish and maintain contained and containing spaces in which the anxieties that prompt such action and reaction can be made more manageable and can be thought about (Solomon, in press). The process of introducing such spaces and processes, through multi-agency working, case discussion, supervision, consultation and other means, necessarily involves uncovering anxieties that have traditionally been defended against. 'The systems we have in place ... are all ways of protecting ourselves from the most primitive anxiety: that of being lost, alone, not knowing ... then any change of working practice must be a breach in our defences and release an enormous amount of stress and anxiety' (Obholzer, 1996, p52). The challenges in implementing changes in policy, such as those proposed in the recent UK Government's White Paper (DCSF, 2008) are clear.

In her study of teachers' perceptions of school exclusion, Elle Rustique-Forrester (2001) concluded that teachers viewed the interaction between schools and national policies as having crucial effects on their classroom practice, with significant implications for exclusion. They cited reduced time and tolerance as impacting on decisions around exclusion, indicating increased paranoid-schizoid functioning over time within those school systems surveyed. The challenge of current and future policy is to safeguard time, tolerance and support for understanding, in the context of other desires and tasks for academic standards in education.

Implications for practice and provision

When reintegration into mainstream school is not possible or appropriate, it is important for this not to be seen as a failure, but rather in terms of appropriate placement. This keeps pupils visible, working explicitly against the tendency to make exclusion systems closed and invisible.

Example

Adam was a 13 year old boy permanently excluded for disruptive behaviour and verbal abuse. His background included separation from his mother and a period of time in care. An assessment over time in the PRU resulted in a recommendation for special (day EBD) provision. Adam himself was keen to attend the identified school, and colleagues worked closely with his mother to support her to accept this. As a result, Adam made a very positive transition to this appropriate placement.

If reintegration and inclusion are to be meaningful for pupils with emotional and behavioural difficulties (Cooper, 2004; O'Hanlon and Thomas, 2004), particularly in terms of social and academic engagement (Cooper, 2005), then society needs to initiate and then mirror such engagement with these young people. A willingness to engage with these pupils and their families, individually in schools and more generally in society and through policy, offers a possibility of safety and security, containment and understanding, hope and the possibility of change and transformation in people's lives. This means there needs to be access to a range of opportunities to meet pupils' diverse needs. A diverse range of educational, psychological, safeguarding and social care services and provision needs to be available, to ensure the promotion of pupils' engagement, while conditions are created and maintained in which professionals and services can strive to think about and understand pupils' needs, in order to promote their psychic reintegration. I would argue that genuine multi-agency practice offers the possibility of such understanding (Solomon, in press).

Conclusion

Re-integration can have different meanings – educationally and psychologically. At its heart must lie the possibility of understanding, in settings and contexts that offer children and families containment, integration and hope. Such emotional and psychic integration is what underpins education and learning – in whatever setting. The capacity for thinking, curiosity and understanding is severely threatened when unconscious societal pressures pull all of us towards judging, splitting and evacuation. Only by holding on to our capacities, and supporting each other to do so, can we offer hope to those vulnerable children and families who find themselves on the margins of our society and our education system. To turn John Major's comment on its head, 'It is time to understand a little more, and condemn a little less'.

Note: This chapter is based on a paper given at a conference held at the Tavistock Clinic, London, in March 2008, entitled 'School Exclusion: Psychological Perspectives'.

All names of pupils and teachers have been changed.

PART 2
Case Examples

Introduction to the case examples

During the course of our professional lives the authors have had numerous contacts with schools and families that have been affected by exclusion. In one way we are privileged, because we have access to both the family and the institution. It occurred to us, however, that we often did not see the big picture when an exclusion happened, because our time was often taken up dealing with just one aspect of a case. When this happened, it was easy to ignore or minimise the experiences of others involved. We were curious, therefore, about what this 'big picture' might look like. The case examples presented in this chapter represent our attempt to do this. We have chosen to illuminate the process of exclusion from school by asking a number of key individuals to tell their stories.

Our approach to researching exclusion from school is underpinned by some key concepts about objectivity and subjectivity. The word research might bring to mind an image of a laboratory experiment in which we manipulate or change things under controlled conditions in order to observe the effects of our changes. This type of approach might be useful if we are dealing with inanimate objects whose properties remain constant. For example, we know that if we apply a heat source to water it will boil when the temperature reaches 100^0 Centigrade. We know that the boiling point will be affected by atmospheric pressure, but because we know the rules about the relationship between boiling point and pressure we can predict with a great amount of certainty what the boiling point will be under specific atmospheric conditions. Here, then, we are working with predictable cause and effect relationships.

In this world, knowledge is about being objective and scientific. We assume that reality is something that is subject to predictable rules and can therefore be measured objectively. This might be true if we are looking at boiling water. Whether water boils or not is not dependent on matters such as the day of the week, the time of day or whether the water feels like boiling or not.

This point leads us to consider how we apply the notion of research when we are working with people. Each human being has his or her own thoughts, feelings and opinions. Who we are and how we think are shaped by how we experience the world (although we do of course acknowledge that there are aspects of our biological inheritance that play a part as well). Therefore, our definition of what is real or true might differ from your definition. This is what *subjectivity* is about. In this world, therefore, knowledge is about our subjective experience. It could be argued that there are as many right answers to questions about truth and reality as there are people. Returning to the notion of research, then, we can see that trying to treat people as subjects of experiments might be problematic. So, when we are asking questions about something like exclusion from school we are not going to be able to come up with some neatly packaged theory about what causes children and young people to be excluded from school. The reason for this is that we are not dealing with the predictable. For each child or young person excluded from school there is a unique set of circumstances surrounding the exclusion.

You might then be tempted to enquire 'why bother?' if it doesn't seem possible to uncover the causes of exclusion. However, research in the educational and social science arena isn't necessarily concerned with looking at cause and effect because there is a recognition that when our subjects are people we are not going to be able to reduce life experiences to a set of simple, predictable relationships and events. So in justifying why we do bother, it's important to see this project as part of a contribution to a body of knowledge about exclusion. This body of knowledge might tell us something about patterns or trends related to exclusion, which in turn might help us to think about ways to prevent it or to deal with it more effectively. Just because we are dealing with the subjective doesn't mean that life is a random experience that isn't worth investigating. What we aren't trying to show is that there is one objective truth about exclusion that can be applied in all cases. Life simply isn't like that.

A recognition that research involving people somehow needs to be different from a laboratory experiment has led to a proliferation of different ways of doing research. We have chosen an approach called *phenomenology*. This book gives the accounts of those who have been excluded from schools in the United Kingdom in the twenty first century. The accounts are told verbatim from the participant's perspective. Accordingly, it is an application of phenomenology to this field. We will go on to describe this approach briefly, in order to give readers a context for the way in which we researched our project. We take as our starting point a definition of phenomenology that we think encapsulates our approach to school exclusion: 'phenomenological research is expressly interested in people's experiences and particularly the experiences of those people who are usually ignored.' (Levering, 2006, p457). We would argue that our approach to examining exclusion from school does incorporate the views of the ignored, because we include the accounts of the excluded pupil and his or her parent(s).

Phenomenology has its roots in philosophy, via the work of two principal theorists, Edmund Husserl (1859-1938) and one of his students, Martin Heidegger (1889-1976). Husserl is sometimes called the 'father of phenomenology' because he incorporated the concepts into a unified theory. Husserl uses the term 'Lebenswelt' (Husserl, 1936), translated as 'lived experience' and emphasises that phenomenology involves describing experiences. Husserl's phenomenology, as applied to research, emphasises that the researcher should have few preconceptions and should look at common features of lived experience (Lopez and Willis, 2004). Husserl calls the restraint of preconceptions 'bracketing', a process that involves suspending subjectivity and not making judgements or assumptions.

Interpretation is not a strong feature of Husserl's phenomenology. The interpretive element is a feature of Heidegger's phenomenology. Heidegger introduces the notion of 'Dasein' (1927), and can be translated as 'being in the world'. Dasein is not just about lived experience but involves the meaning of being. He rejected the idea that experience can be 'bracketed' as in Husserls' view, emphasising instead reflection and interpretation of experience. Heidegger argued that it was not possible to be fully objective. So, the relationship to the Lebenswelt rather than the Lebenswelt itself is important in Heidegger's phenomenology.

Phenomenological approaches to research are found particularly in health care and in family therapy. In these contexts, it is important for professionals to understand the way in which individuals experience what might appear to be the same family (in the case of applications in family therapy) or illness (in health related applications). For example, as Dyson (2005) points out, there might be agreement about what asthma is, but this does not mean that it is experienced in exactly the same way by all those people who have this condition. Stubblefield and Murray (2002) use a phenomenological approach to help to understand mental illness. In family therapy, Sprenkle (2005) refers to 'storytelling' as a means of looking at how each member of a family might make sense of a family event: 'just as family therapists do, phenomenological family researchers must elicit the perceptions and views of all family members to get the total picture of a particular family' (p66).

Similarly, our project aimed to elicit the views of a range of individuals involved in one phenomenon: an exclusion from school. We are dealing with two levels or layers, because we are looking at the broad topic of exclusion from school via a number of case examples (a macro level), but within each case example we are uncovering what exclusion means to a number of key individuals involved in one specific exclusion from school (a micro level). The decision to include 'complex discourses' in the title was a deliberate attempt to signal that we are dealing with a multi layered topic.

In order to identify potential participants, we undertook purposive sampling, that is, a sample of participants was obtained by selecting according to specific characteristics. A purposive sample is in keeping with a phenomenological approach, because it was important to choose participants who had experience of the phenomenon that we were interested in, that of exclusion from school. In the case of our research, we were interested in identifying young people who had been excluded from a school. There was a certain amount of hand picking of the sample. Although the scope of the research did not permit use of a large representative sample, we nevertheless made sure that our participants were male and female and from more than one ethnic background. There was also a practical aspect, in that from the initial identification of potential participants there were some who did not wish to take part or who agreed initially and then withdrew or simply avoided contact with the authors. These cases were not followed up. None of the participants was offered any inducement or reward for taking part.

In terms of research methods associated with phenomenology, the principal method is that of the unstructured interview. This method allows the participant to recount their experiences without any boundaries imposed by the researcher, which would be the case if the interviews were structured; that is, an interview with 'a standard format of pre-determined questions in a set order' or semi structured that is, interviews that 'involve the interviewer deciding in advance what broad topics are to be covered and what main questions are to be asked' (Miller and Brewer, 2003, p167).

As we have seen, phenomenology is primarily concerned with stories or accounts of experiences, thus a method that allows the participant 'free rein' in terms of recounting their experiences is appropriate. We have used this method in our research. However, we have also asked participants to comment and reflect on their experiences, adding an extra dimension to the descriptions that Denscome (2003) emphasises in phenomenological research.

We therefore carried out unstructured interviews with key individuals involved in an exclusion: the pupil, the parent, a representative from the excluding school and a representative from the Pupil Referral Unit (PRU). Some case examples include additional interviews with other individuals such as learning mentors. The interviews were recorded and transcribed. Each account was then edited in order to give some structure and progression and to eliminate repetition. However, the words that are reproduced are the *participants' own* words. We have not altered their words at all.

Turning to the issue of analysis and interpretation, we have followed a Husserlian view and taken a very light touch approach. We have not tried to carry out a detailed analysis because we feel that this would defeat the object of having the accounts as the centrepiece of the book. For example, in phenomenological research, Groenewald (2004) comments that the notion of 'data analysis' might be seen as running counter to the phenomenological approach, because analysis implies a breaking down of data which then might interfere with presenting the phenomenon. Groenewald prefers the term 'explicitation'.

The small number of examples that we have included cannot be seen as representing school exclusion; therefore our pragmatic view is that even if we did analyse and interpret in detail, this would not make the findings more valid. Our aim is to illuminate, not to explain or generalise. However, we have given some thought to the examples and have followed Giorgi's (1994) three steps for a phenomenological method:

- description: giving a precise account

- reduction: the researcher takes a step back from the topic (similar to the process of bracketing); and

- search for essences: where the characteristics of the phenomenon are examined so that 'essential' characteristics are identified

We have therefore attempted in the final chapter to identify some common characteristics of the case examples and have used these to suggest ways in which these characteristics might be helpful in identifying some future directions for school exclusion or, as Todres and Wheeler (2001) comment: 'the task of phenomenology is to clarify the 'life world'' (p3).

A note about ethical issues

Throughout the project we have referred to guidance from the British Psychological Society (BPS, 2004) and the British Educational Research Association

(BERA, 2004). We have ensured that informed voluntary consent is obtained and that complete confidentiality is maintained. We have used the guidance to inform the conduct of our research in relation to work with vulnerable individuals, since our research involves interviews about a traumatic event with young people under the age of 18.

In accordance with the guidelines detailed above, the case examples presented have been anonymised so that none of the participants can be identified. However, we realised that each participant reading the case example would be able to recognise themselves and would therefore be able to identify the other contributors. This raised issues about the information that each individual offered about a particular case, because there was potential for causing hurt or offence if one participant disagreed with the views of another, or with the particular way in which the circumstances of an exclusion were described.

We have addressed this issue by having a two tier approach to obtaining consent of participants. Initially, we obtained consent to carry out the interview and to tape record it. Each participant was then sent a copy of the transcript of their interview so that they could give some initial feedback about any material that they would prefer not to be included in the final edited case example. After each case example had been edited, each participant was sent the entire write up; that is, they received the edited interviews of all those involved. At this stage, participants were able to ask for any material to be removed that they considered untrue or that they felt uncomfortable about being in print. The authors agreed to remove any material without question. After this opportunity had been offered and any action requested taken, participants were asked to sign a consent form agreeing to the case example being included in the book. Once the consent form was signed, no alterations were made to the case examples. In the case of the pupil (all pupils were under the age of 18), we obtained consent from the pupil and from his or her parent(s).

The process of sending both individual transcripts and edited case examples back to all participants had the added benefit of addressing validity, or what Groenewald refers to as 'validity and truthfulness' in phenomenological research. Participants had an opportunity to see what they had said and to reflect on it and then, if they felt it appropriate, to give feedback to the authors. Therefore, this additional step to address the ethical issues has also helped to increase confidence that the accounts are authentic.

3

Letitia

L etitia is a dual heritage African Caribbean/white British girl. She was permanently excluded from a High School (referred to as Daffodil High School) during Year 9. This was her second High School. She left her first High School (referred to as Primrose High School) during Year 8 due to increasing difficulties that might have resulted in an exclusion had her mother not decided to move her. Letitia is the youngest of four children. None of her siblings has experienced difficulties in school that resulted in any fixed term or permanent exclusions. Letitia's mother is a single parent.

Letitia's account of her exclusion
Letitia's description of the exclusion, Governor's meeting and placement at the PRU

I started at Primrose High School in Year 7, everything was alright for the first few months, and then I came to the end of Year 7 and I was just getting blamed for things and come back after and I kept getting excluded for like keep getting sent out of lessons, being cheeky to teachers so after that my mom said just move, so I had a move to Daffodil High School, it started off alright but then I started getting into trouble for things I didn't do and for things that I did do.

Things started to become more serious like threatening teachers they were saying that I had done and just things like that and then they kept excluding me. So then there was an incident where some dinner ladies said I couldn't go to the dinner hall for one day so after the weekend I went back up there and they said I couldn't go there permanently but I didn't know that so then I got into trouble for that but when I was trying to ask why I was getting into trouble because I didn't know it started into an argument and then I ended up walking out of school and they permanently excluded me for that and that was it.

[At the Governor's meeting]

There was me and my mom on one side of the table and there was about ten teachers on the other side and the Governors at the side and they tried to, they were putting across all their stuff on their paper and then they brought up a robbery, but it wasn't robbery because I didn't do it and they just expected it though and they had excluded me and when my mom, right, said that's not how it went the teachers were trying to argue the case back and stuff like that. Just I felt small and everybody was just throwing things at me no positive stuff.

[At Wordsworth House, the PRU]

That was good there but I just didn't enjoy it. Just the other pupils that were there just weren't like me, I just didn't really speak to no one there.

Letitia's feelings about her exclusion
I wish I could go back and change it. I weren't treated properly but I put up with it. I came from Daffodil High School to Primrose High School they said they were going to put some support in for me, but I never had none of that and then when we had a meeting with my mom they said they were going to put in a mentor and for my mentor to come in, but they never paid for Michelle to come in and they never give me a mentor. There was only my Head of House but she wasn't supposed to support me, but she did anyway. She got me a timeout card, if I needed anything she told me to come to her. She tried to get Michelle in and she spoke to my mom like on a regular basis. Anything that happened in the week I could go back to her [Michelle] and she would speak about it with me and then talk about it to the teachers after and it would have been sorted. They need to contact the parents at an earlier stage and do what they are supposed to do.

Letitia's mother's account of her exclusion
Letitia's mother outlines events and circumstances leading up to the first instances of difficult behaviour at High School
Basically throughout Primary school Letitia was fine. There was no issues, she did well in her schoolwork, musically she did well, she played the cello, she didn't get in any trouble. Then she went to High School. It was around the same time as me and her dad split up so I don't know if that has any bearing on her behaviour, I personally think it has. Right from within a couple of months she was having problems at Primrose High School. Teachers were ringing me to go into the school for meetings and I attended all the meetings. I was quite frank and honest with them about the issues that had been going on because there was quite a lot of personal issues that went on at that time and you don't particularly want to talk about it but I went

up there and talked to the teachers about the issues with Letitia's dad and I thought they would take that on board and help.

Things didn't improve. Her behaviour became worse and it was like mainly cheekiness, didn't like authority, didn't like people shouting at her so she would lose her temper and shout back and so she started off with detentions. I mean I can't even remember the reason for the first exclusion because she has had many. To be honest with you I think it was over something really stupid that they had no alternative because things hadn't improved but it wasn't over something dangerous or fighting or drugs or anything. It was cheekiness or general misbehaviour. When they excluded her they said we have had this many sleuth reports over the last week and we have no alternative but to exclude her. I dunno what that meant.

Letitia's mother describes the steps she took to obtain support for Letitia and the provision put in place at her school

I kept saying I think she needs some counselling or something, I really believed at the time because her behaviour at home was quite bad as well, like the way she spoke to me, she wouldn't do as she was told, I was beginning to get very worried about things she was doing because I was thinking you know she's only 12, and she was quite at risk. She would disappear and I wouldn't know where she had gone, the one time she had been drinking so there were issues at home as well. I went to my own GP and I said I think she needs some counselling and I said can we get her referred to CAMHS [Child and Adolescent Mental Health Service] or something? The doctor told me I would need a letter from the school. I went to the school and I asked them to send a letter which they did and I wrote a letter to the doctor as well and he said OK I'll make the referral and up until this day we have never had anything come back off that!

Primrose High School put her into Michael Court [an offsite provision for pupils in danger of exclusion, attended for a short period of time]. They said it's OK we'll pay for her, this will sort her out, I said OK then, and she went to Michael Court for about 4 or 5 weeks before the summer holidays. They said right after they have been to Michael Court they get support after. That didn't happen because they broke up for the summer holidays. She went back, started getting into trouble again so I said well where is this support from Michael Court that was promised? I was trying to contact Michael Court and I couldn't get them on the phone at all. I was saying to the school you have spent a lot of money sending her to Michael Court, there's issues still and you can't be bothered to follow it up when you have paid for a service which cost about £800. Nothing ever came of that, that wasn't followed through.

We had a report come in at work about the Children's Fund, so I rang up a counselling service and said look you know I think she needs some counselling. They said yes we'll do an assessment on her. We went for an appointment they said yes she's suitable for the counselling and then I was waiting ages, they had a waiting list basically. So during that time things got worse and counselling never came through.

I think I had something come through the post about services that support children and I saw this transition service for Afro-Caribbean children. I rang up and spoke to Michelle, explained my situation and I said look I'm really desperate I really need some help because I don't seem to be getting it from anywhere, so Michelle agreed to become involved and she did start working with Letitia at Primrose High School.

Letitia's mother describes the change of school in Year 8

Things deteriorated, the school suggested that perhaps I should consider moving schools and I was beginning to think I needed to move her school before she was excluded so I applied to move her to Daffodil High School. I tried to change the school to Daffodil High School. I put the form in, had a phone call from education because I put a long letter in with this form saying she was at high risk of exclusion, she needs support. They said that really we should be treated as a managed move so I said OK what's the difference between me requesting a move and a managed move? A managed move is managed between schools and that means that Letitia will move and have money attached to her to get support so I said that's great, if that's gonna get support then we'll do it that way. That was in the November, end of December I still didn't hear anything and things were getting worse at Primrose High School. In fact I was keeping her off school some days. If I thought 'today she's gonna get in trouble' I didn't send her.

When I rang up to chase up the managed move they said that won't be looking at any managed moves until after April. So then I said well OK I don't want to go through the managed move route I want you to treat my application as I sent it in. So then they came back to me and said they refused to change the school because there was no places [at Daffodil High School]. So I had to appeal. I won that appeal because it was true they hadn't treated it properly. I won my appeal and that meant that she could go to Daffodil High School so I went to Daffodil High School, well I rang up Daffodil High School and said I need to speak to somebody before she starts, tell them what the issues were and that happened and they told me at first she was going to the Larkin Road site, so I went and saw a teacher there, I can't remember her name now, and told her the full story and, yeah OK we'll make sure that support is put in place and all the rest of it, and then when the letter came through for her to start she had got to start at the other site which is Edward Road, I said OK.

So I went to the school with her on the first day to see somebody else and I explained look this is what is happening and also Michelle is supporting her can she continue to support her here? And at the same time, not long after she had started at Daffodil High School I chased up the counselling service and they were in a position to start seeing her so I told the school and I said the counselling service need to come in to see Letitia so obviously they needed to be able to do that and Michelle needed to come in on a weekly basis. Michelle contacted the school, there was issues with that because Michelle, the first few times Michelle went there it was like well who are you and what are you doing here? And it took her about four attempts to actually start seeing Letitia, it was really difficult. The counselling service, Letitia saw them once, and then the appointment that was supposed to come through never got to her so she never got to see anybody and they closed it off. So it wasn't managed very well by the school anyway.

Letitia's mother describes the exclusion from the second High School (Daffodil High School)

Letitia was OK for the first couple of months and then things started going downhill again and I thought well I can't cope with this. If you think about it we went from Year 7 this all happened during Year 8. By the time she started Daffodil High School you are talking about March of Year 8 so she did a few months and then they had the summer holiday and then she was in Year 9. It started with some minor issues which they didn't like at the school and she got into trouble and the teachers began to know. There was one particular teacher there who was really good, who was very supportive and we kept in contact actually and she tried to sort of stick up for Letitia if you like but she wasn't on senior management so she found it quite difficult. Anyway there came a time when Michelle, she had supported her for a few months then when she went back in Year 9, Michelle had to send a letter to the school to say you need to pay for this because she wasn't being funded and the school refused to pay basically, even though I sort of said I think she needs to work with her because it is consistent and they were saying no we have our own in-house schemes and all the rest of it so they wouldn't pay. So Letitia was supposed to have a pastoral mentor there and that didn't happen, I mean she saw this woman once and then Letitia didn't get any more messages to come out of lessons to come and meet her so that didn't happen.

All this time Letitia is getting in bits of trouble, detention – she wouldn't attend detention, she had some arguments with teachers, she walked off site a couple of times, a couple of fixed term suspensions came up because she was accused of a couple of things, I mean a couple of the suspensions I questioned. I mean obviously I went to the school every time and met with all the management and the Head and everybody. She got accused of stealing a mobile phone which was nothing to do with her but that still remained on her record up until she was excluded. It had got theft of mobile phone, which I still don't agree with – she actually got suspended for it as well and they never found that she had taken it – there was no action ever taken and then she got suspended for something else, cheeking a teacher, then she got suspended, her and another group of girls wrote graffiti on the toilets, just some small writing but nevertheless anyway, but they cleaned it off, that was part of the punishment, that was another suspension.

Things just started to get worse again and I was sort of going up the school going look you know I don't know what to do I don't know who to turn to, I can even remember me going to Social Services and saying help! And nobody, oh somebody will ring you back, and nobody ever rang me back and then she ended up being permanently excluded because they said she had had so many exclusions.

Letitia's mother describes attending the Governor's meeting following Letitia's permanent exclusion

She was off for a few weeks before we even went for the meeting, you know when they have to make the final decision with the governors, so I went to that final meeting and Michelle came with me, it was on an evening, and I'm really glad Michelle came with me because we walked in and I couldn't believe it. There was that many people sitting around this table, all the managers, all the Heads, governors there, very intimidating and we sat down and they sort of read out this long list of misdemeanours and we were sitting there. Then I was given a chance to speak and I brought up that I had always been in touch with the school, I had begged for support for Letitia. Mr. Stone who is the manager tried to have an argument on me in the meeting. This is a man who really disliked Letitia. He made a comment in that meeting to say she's a waste of time basically and nobody is ever going to be bothered about her, you know comments like that. I just said I am really shocked that a professional would make comments like that. So he had had his say and when it was time for me and I was sort of saying well the school never did this and Mr. Stone you never did this and whatever, he started getting really defensive and trying to argue with me while I was talking and I had to say to him I'm not being funny but I think you are really rude, I have sat here and let you say what you needed to say now it's my turn to speak.

I just thought I don't know how people cope in meetings like that, you know I am used to sitting in meetings with professionals at work so I know how it works, I know how to put my point across but how do other parents who haven't got that experience manage in that type of environment, it must be really difficult that's what I kept thinking because I really struggled with it. So anyway that was that and I think half way through it Mr Green [head teacher] was probably thinking oh it doesn't look too good here because we haven't done all these things and we have excluded her permanently, so he kept saying to Letitia, Letitia what about if we give you another chance would you come back? Well Letitia had already made up her mind after that four weeks off – I'm not going back there Mr. Stone is gunning for me, it doesn't matter what I do he's gonna pick on me. Letitia says no I don't want to come back. Anyway we had to go outside while the governors all had a confab and when we went back in the governors said that if Letitia was willing to go back they would have overturned that exclusion. They did turn round and say to the school you know you have not done this you have not done that you should have done this so they sort of got a bit of a dressing down in that meeting. So that was that, Letitia was excluded permanently.

Letitia's mother reflects on the experience of dealing with Letitia's exclusion

You know I have been stressed out by it all since Year 7. I have had time off work, it's a good job they are understanding, I could have lost my job. You wouldn't believe I've had to come out, you know I've been pulled out of work and everything. I had to take a lot of time off to sort things out, you know going to appeals, going to meetings. So basically it was very stressful for me and I don't think I am a stupid person or a thick person and you know I'm used to dealing with professional people and I really don't know how some parents who haven't got that experience cope with the whole system, with everything, the meetings, the school, education, going through appeals. I would go up the school and I felt that if I had been the type of parent who ignored the school and Letitia hadn't got high educational attainment or if I beat her up or something I would have support thrown at me but I just felt that there was nothing, no support there at all and I was having to search out support for myself.

One of the things I have sort of noticed is that the schools are very big now I mean you know a thousand and odd pupils, it's not like years ago when you had small schools with smaller numbers so I know it's difficult to manage a large school and it's difficult to hone in on an individual, do you know what I mean? But that's no good to the child is it? The fact that they are in a large school and people haven't got time, it is not good enough I don't think. That's the one thing, the other thing is there's a lot of people who can make decisions within schools so Letitia wasn't excluded by one person it was always you know the exclusion decision might have been made by the manager but it was always a teacher coming across with a load of stuff or another teacher coming across and there's so many people involved who have got authority if you like and who can impact on whether somebody gets excluded a teacher might not understand what is going on with that child or do you know what

I mean? And might not take that into consideration before putting a report in so I just find the whole thing is not managed well and I just can't believe it when children are children and they are supposed to be vulnerable, you know they are classed as vulnerable people aren't they? And I found that within schools, you know like I say, they would agree to something and that's why I say it's lip service, because to me it's like we agreed to that so we've ticked that box but they have never really tried to make it work by saying OK she's got problems, she's not going to change overnight but we need to not suspend her again during this period unless she does something dangerous or really you know, do you know what I mean?

So you know the whole experience to me has been vile and I can't wait for her to leave school 'cos I feel then a lot of the stress will be off her. Well me being selfish I just talk about how it's affected me without even how it's impacted on Letitia. Letitia had got to the point where she had no confidence in herself. Nobody was praising her for anything she did good it was all about bad Letitia or that Letitia again and I have had to work really hard with her. She's not an angel but things have improved massively and we have had to work really, really hard.

So I try really, really hard to bring her up properly and she's a nightmare. That's the story really in a nutshell I mean to be honest I could probably write a whole book on it myself, my whole experience 'cos like everything was stressful.

The mentor's account of Letitia's exclusion
Michelle is a mentor employed by the African Caribbean Resource Centre. She supported Letitia in both her High Schools and in the PRU. M gives her thoughts about Letitias exclusion and then reflects on some of the issues raised in relation to the needs of African Caribbean pupils.

I met Letitia about two years ago. I met her because the school identified her as somebody who needs help even though she was considered bright and intelligent she was not moving on. I got her on a one to one basis and tried to figure out why she was not progressing and why she was not getting on in school. Most of the problems stemmed around her relationships with the teachers, she didn't get on with them, some she did most she didn't, and of course if you don't get along with your teachers you are not very happy at school and so we tried to work on things like confidence, self-esteem and anger, anger management and I put some programmes together to try to get her to realise when she gets angry and why she gets angry and how to treat the situation when she gets angry. They started working a little bit but then sometimes when she gets really off the rails she would forget everything we were doing there and she will just do everything we said not to do. Then she kept insisting she wanted to leave the school because she was not getting on and mom thought it was best that she moved and we organised a managed move for her to another school.

She went to Daffodil High School following Primrose High School. At first they [Daffodil High School] were receptive to the idea of me helping her with the transition from one school to the other and as we went through the transition period she started doing a little better. There were a couple of instances where she fell out with teachers but initially she started doing OK and she started developing a relationship with one of the teachers there. Then when my transition period was over because Daffodil High School is out of our remit, they had to actually pay in order to have me stay on. Mom wanted me to stay on but Daffodil High School never really replied to any of our requests to have me stay on and I couldn't really keep going there and not getting paid for it. So I had to discontinue our one to one sessions. I hadn't seen her for a while and then mom called me and said can I come with her to an exclusions meeting. I was really sad because I felt like it could have been a really good start for her, but it just didn't work out that way.

At the meeting when she was eventually excluded I don't think that the governors wanted to exclude her, they asked about four times 'do you want to stay?' In other words we can let you stay here, but each time she said no I want to go I want to get out. I think the way some of the teachers treated her she felt like 'I can't stay there, I don't want to stay there' and she kept saying 'no I don't want to stay there I want to go'. Then of course she had to go to a Pupil Referral Unit [PRU]. She didn't want to be in the PRU and so she truanted and I only got with her a limited amount of time. There was a possibility that because she truanted so many times she may not get into a mainstream school but I also know that the PRU head teacher was trying to get her straight into college and to do something practical which is probably what she wants.

I think that one of the issues that I had difficulty with Letitia is the way in which she spoke to people. I think sometimes with the pressure of teaching and accountability that teachers are under, they come into a class and they expect compliance and not all the children are going to fit into a system like that especially, and I have to say especially black minority children, the system is not suited for them anyhow. She did not like the way in which they used their power against her, that's how she saw it I think and so anything that they said she would snap back. I think it was misinterpreted as her being rude and of course they would answer back reacting to her. Then she would rebel, she would either not turn up for class or not turn up for school or not do her work or make an excuse which of course that didn't go down well with her teachers.

Michelle's reflections about exclusion and ethnic minority pupils

Well personally I think that unfortunately in the UK, the majority of children who are fixed term and permanently excluded are black and minority students but they are mainly, even though you have the other minorities like Asian, they are mainly African and African-Caribbean children, or children like Letitia who are dual heritage. I thought about it and I think that the legislation is there to help them but I think that in the society, in people's minds, they still look at ethnic minority or African and African-Caribbean children or people in a negative way. I think that teachers on the whole don't understand the contribution that black people have made to this society and because they don't understand it or they don't know it or they have not been taught it so therefore they don't see the black child as important. I recently went to speak to one of the teachers of one of the students that I am helping. She looked down at me, she spoke down to me and I am talking to her from one professional to another and I am adult and I was amazed at her rudeness. She even raised her voice at me and I went the other way deliberately so that I would not raise my voice. What I was trying to do was to negotiate for this child to come and see me at the same time to be in her class and she was not having it at all. She did not see the need to help this child.

Black children react differently to things. I will go to a black student and I will speak to them and I will mainly hold them by the arm and say 'how you doing?'. If somebody else from another culture do that to a black student they would be like 'why are you touching me?' because they don't understand when somebody from another culture do it because to them it is always a negative thing. Also the way they move, the way they talk, the way they joke, they will joke and they will be going back and forth to each other joking and if you don't know and understand the culture you would think they are having an argument but it's banter between them. When the children are at home they are living the Caribbean lifestyle. It's a different culture, they speak a different language. Some of them speak Patois when they are at home but then when they come into the school system, where they can't speak Patois, they can't laugh and joke the way their moms and dads and their uncles laugh and joke because that is considered a no-no and you are sent into isolation for it, they feel suppressed.

It's High Schools particularly, on the whole statistics show that black children excel up to Primary, when they hit High School they do badly. The High School system is very 'you'd better comply or else'. We are not a people like that, we are very laid back, we will get things done but we will get things done in a different way and there is a misunderstanding and I know unwillingness to appreciate that. Society is not afraid to demonise the black child which is very, very terrifying for them and it's not very encouraging at all and there are some people who are just racist. There are

60

black children, I will put my hand up and say who are rude. I walk the corridor at schools and I have heard white children swearing the ugliest words and I hear a black child either saying the same thing or not as bad and they get shouted at and I am like 'what's the difference?'.

Recently I sat in a class in this case it was a little Asian young lad, and he was fidgeting but then there was a white child in the back who was getting up and walking around in the back and I think he obviously had some special needs or something but I think the little one in front maybe had special needs too and the teacher put the little Asian boy outside, put him outside the class and the little white boy she didn't do anything about it and I sat there and I thought 'alright then, that's interesting isn't it', and the little one was doing less than the one in the back. Is that fair?

The other issue for boys is black masculinity. The black boys are coming into their own when they are 11, 12, 13 and there are certain things they do not like for people to come up in their face and talk to them. They want you to respect them and when you disrespect then they disrespect you as well. And of course there is on the one side now the pressure of the gangs and being liked, these gangland people want them as well, they are under a lot of pressure.

I think that teachers do not believe that black students can achieve and again I think it's because they don't realise how much black people have contributed to this society. I was just looking, together with my group in a school, at a DVD produced by the Open University about how slaves built a castle. Slave labour was used to build castles and abbeys in England, and they were surprised at that. They didn't realise, when you walk up to these historical places it's the slave labour in the Caribbean and the slave labour here that helped contribute to this. You have a place in this society and they were surprised – you could see the difference in their faces 'you mean our forefathers contributed?' – I said 'yes' – and I think teachers are not aware of that and they don't like it when we come into the school to actually tell the children this.

Black history is really important. Teachers need to know it and the children need to know it and a lot of the children born here don't know it. Because let's face it, the white children know where their great grandmother, their grandmother is from and a black child thinks 'oh, somewhere in the Caribbean, Africa – I don't know', they don't know where they come from where they are going so therefore they are uncertain and of course if they have people who don't know either telling them what you should do is actually be a singer or a runner and nothing else, you can't be a doctor, a lawyer, a scientist then they believe it. We suppress the black children and I don't understand that. I took my children to the Caribbean for seven months and my husband would say I can't believe that there are so many black people on TV. I told my son, I said and guess who runs the country and he was like 'oh yeah a black prime minister' and he asked 'can I be prime minister?' I said 'yeah of course you can be prime minister' and this is after arriving a few weeks in the Caribbean. He would never say that to me here. He figured it out after a few weeks, he wouldn't say that here.

The PRU manager's account

It was made known to us that Letitia had had a managed move from one school to another and then from the school she had been managed to she was excluded and the reason for that exclusion was persistent disruption and defiance, mostly defiance. It was explained to us that one of the things that Letitia did was argue face to face with members of staff in front of other pupils in the classroom and defied them and refused to attend or walk off site. That caused significant disruption in the class and prevented others from learning. After a series of situations like this she was given the ultimate consequence which is exclusion. Following her arrival here we delved into matters a little further and discovered that the Head of the school she was excluded from actually gave her, during the exclusion meeting, four chances to agree to abide by the rules of the school and she would be allowed back. On each of the four occasions she refused to agree to that and left the Head with no option but to exclude her and from that we gathered that she may well present as being quite stubborn.

Initially Letitia refused to attend, she came with her mother for interview but she didn't turn up on the first day or the second day. We had to pursue the matter with the Education Welfare Officer, we had quite a difficult time over the first week just getting her here at all. She didn't present as being particularly defiant face to face, she simply voted with her feet and refused to come. It was at that point where we basically said you really will need to come, if you don't attend you will be in the unfortunate situation where you will end up having the Education Welfare Officers at your door every day, etc. Anyway it seemed to put enough pressure on her to encourage her to come but she still left this site on a couple of occasions without permission. She was then addressed in simple face to face conversations, but we also realised this is an intelligent young lady, she was predicted to get quite high grades although our baseline assessments indicate that they are not as high as the school had suggested. From that we have measured what she is capable of rather than what her potential is and that she has a barrier to learning as she wants to learn her way in her time and not what people tell her to do and that is what we have observed with her.

So we recognised her need and we have negotiated the position whereby she does come in here for some half days and then she goes home with her computer. What we have done is develop a trusting relationship, she has done what we asked her to do. We then offered her a part-time timetable here and part-time at home we wanted to allow her that time away from this environment. It has also developed as a significant level of trust, she now knows we keep our word. I don't believe she is ready to return to mainstream school yet, but with limited time I would not feel that Key Stage 4 PRU would be appropriate. Her immediate response to her exit school [that is the school she will attend after her time in the PRU] was 'I am not going there' and again very typical of a lot of kids who make this decision based on absolutely no information whatsoever, she's never been in the school, she's never visited it in any way shape or form, she doesn't know what goes on there.

The PRU manager's reflections on changes that might help Letitia to return to a mainstream school

I think the amount of work that is necessary to make this young lady ready for learning is quite significant. I think many of the problems that we have to address are based around issues that are outside of education. Creating a different environment than school, smaller groups, almost like a college with no uniform necessary, just another area of bureaucracy that we can do without, a relaxed situation, trusting, more open situation. Preferably an environment where she will have some degree of control over her own education so where the young people are actually involved in leading the school as it were. Instead of having something done to her she is involved in having someone doing something with her. That's the sort of environment she needs.

The school's account
The school's account of Letitia's exclusion is provided by Trevor, a senior member of staff with responsibility for pastoral care at the school designated Daffodil High School in previous interviews

Letitia joined us towards the end of Year 8. She came through as a normal admission through mum asking for a transfer which was granted by the Admissions department. However, in reality she should have perhaps come on a school sponsored managed transfer, which I think Primrose High School would have agreed with. It came through when we talked to mum that she wasn't really happy with the way that things had been dealt with at Primrose High School. Towards the end of Year 7 she was sent to Michael Court for a two or three week block placement. Mum felt that this was at the wrong time for her because there was no opportunity then for any follow up work to be done because of the six week holiday. So that was, not a waste of time, but there was no opportunity or scope really for any sort of feedback from that and I think then during her time in Year 8 at Primrose High School things escalated and mum took the decision that she was going to move her to us.

So she joined us. Initially she didn't present a problem; she was a bright, very bright, intelligent young lady. From reading through the very limited information that we received on the admission, we placed her with the strongest form tutor that we had so that obviously from a pastoral perspective we knew that Ms C would keep an eye on her and her behaviours. She started off you know, quite well, didn't really present any problems and then towards the beginning of Year 9 started to display some of her previous behaviours. I think at that point she had stopped being supported by Michelle who was her mentor at the time, she came for a few sessions and a few visits when she first moved from Primrose High School. I think at that point then she then started to display behaviours which obviously were unacceptable to us, she would be disruptive in lessons, she was racist towards a supply teacher, there was an incident where a phone was stolen that Letitia was involved in and then it culminated with an unpleasant episode in the dining room where at the top of her voice she shouted 'F*** you' or something like that towards one of the dinner ladies and was quite unpleasant. Previously to that obviously we had given her some periods of fixed term exclusions to try and modify her behaviour.

In the January before she was permanently excluded she was presented at a Governors disciplinary panel and given a final warning as to her behaviour. Both mum and sister attended and were I would say relatively supportive of the school and they had their questions and their own points of view, but obviously when you've got a school with 1600 students then you've obviously got to make your stand against poor behaviour which unfortunately, as intelligent as she was, Letitia did display poor behaviour unfortunately.

In terms of support for Letitia in school, she would have been put on the Special Needs Register at School Action or School Action Plus. She would have had some support from the Special Educational Needs Department. The assistant Head of House worked very very closely with Letitia almost as a mentor, to try and keep her on the straight and narrow. It was just unfortunate that Letitia didn't really respond, she was if you like, I would say pretty much a leader in the sense that she took other girls with her who got themselves into trouble at the same time, but since Letitia has gone, those girls haven't really displayed any of the same kinds of behaviour.

Reflections about Letitia's exclusion and the process of exclusion generally

Letitia was very much a leader to Caribbean girls, and whereas they weren't angels, but they seemed to follow Letitia as a negative role model if you like. I don't know whether those are quite the traits that she already picked up in her two years at Primrose High School or whether she came into a new school and felt that she had to be top dog. A small environment, probably only about 100 students in the year groups so she would have got to have known everybody very quickly, but wasn't as if it was a large year group, she became known almost as soon as she came through the door. I just think it was a shame because she is a very bright young girl and it's a shame that she's had if you like, two failures in mainstream school and I would hope that she manages to survive at the school she's at now, because there's definitely a brain in there and the energies need challenging into the correct direction.

We don't take the decision to permanently exclude anybody lightly. And they have to have reached a tremendous level of poor behaviour for us to do that. Nobody wants to have a stigma of a permanent exclusion attached to them, and we certainly actively seek other ways in which to combat that now. Whether it's onsite provision for students, whether it's a reduced timetable, vocational qualifications because personalisation is a key thing at the moment. One size doesn't fit all for students by any stretch of the imagination. I think it might be that schools, not just this school, but schools in general have to look very carefully in the future at providing almost individual timetables for a small number of students, not every student, but a small number of students who have needs which are different from others.

4

Chip

Chip is 13. He is a white British male. He is the second of three children. His father now lives away with another partner. Chip's older brother was in trouble with the police after the separation, but is now in college. Chip's younger sister is doing well at school. Chip attended five junior schools and was excluded at the end of year 6. Although he started at the secondary school, he was extremely disruptive in class and was sent to the in-school unit. He was disruptive there and was sent to a scheme for difficult pupils. The course finished and he returned to school and he was then permanently excluded.

He was sent to a pupil referral unit, but didn't attend. Instead he started to steal metal from roofs and sell it to scrap dealers. His family lived in rented accommodation. The landlord complained that the house was being damaged and that he would evict the family.

Chip was offered support from a range of sources including teachers, social workers and psychologists. Chip declined to explain his story verbally, but chose to draw a picture of his memory of the mainstream school from which he was permanently excluded.

Chip's mother was in considerable debt. She was offered parenting courses and support from social workers, welfare officers, teachers, psychologists and parent partnership services.

This account tells the story of Chip from the different perspectives of those around him including his mother, teachers and parent partnership workers.

It reveals a degree of complexity and stress that would be difficult to find in other environments in which children are raised.

Interview 1 – The mother

Interviewer

We are here to talk about Chip in particular. What I want to do is just to take you right the way back almost to before the time that Chip was born, the time if you like when Chip was conceived, when you decided to have a child. Did you have any other kids?

Mum

Just one, my eldest, Bill.

Interviewer

... and who were you living with at the time?

Mum

His dad, John.

Interviewer

Can you remember what the circumstances were? Did you decide to have Chip?

Mum

I had been trying, I thought that I could never have no more after my eldest and I had to go and have tests and everything, but everything was fine and then I found out that I was pregnant.

Interviewer

Were you happy about that?

Mum

I was in the beginning but then I found out that John was cheating on me at that time, while I was pregnant with Chip, then when I had Chip, I don't know, I think the first few weeks I wished I hadn't have had him. I remember telling my sister I wished I had never got pregnant.

Interviewer

How did you find out that John was cheating?

Mum

I had a letter pushed through my door to say, no she came to the house first to say that she had been seeing him and like Chip was three months old, and I had a letter pushed through saying that she had just give birth to a son, John's. Then I had maintenance letters come for him.

Interviewer

What did John say? Did he admit it?

Mum

Yes, he admitted to that.

Interviewer

So what happened then?

Mum

We moved. That is a lot of the reason we have moved as many times as we have because I didn't want to stay in the area so we moved.

Interviewer

Did you all stay together?

Mum

Yes. There was Bill, Chip and me.

Interviewer

And John?

Mum

Yes.

Interviewer

Then you had another child?

Mum

Tanya.

Interviewer

How did that come about?

Mum

That was just an accident, but I was happy because it was the family completed then, a daughter, and that's when I decided I was going to be sterilised because John wouldn't and I knew I didn't want any more kids so I was sterilised.

Interviewer

Just talk me through the early years of your family.

Mum

We moved after Chip was born. John was like working doing things that he shouldn't be doing, going out thieving, things like that. Going out catching birds, something else he wasn't supposed to be doing!

Interviewer

Catching birds?

Mum

Yes, you know wild birds, he used to go out catching them and then selling them.

Interviewer

Oh right, was there a market in that?

Mum

There was at that time. I just thought everything was OK but then he started going out drinking more, I think that time he met somebody else again and just went downhill after that.

Interviewer

So what happened after that?

Mum

We moved again. I mean basically we just kept moving trying to, at that time John, I know I had a life with him, but I just wanted John and the kids, that was it, so we just moved again. Then the last time I had just had enough and I told him I wanted a divorce. That was it. The kids were bad at first, they used to cry after him and that but at that time he wasn't bothered.

Interviewer

How old was Chip at that time?

Mum

Well he's got to have been about 4 or 5 something like that.

Interviewer

And did John go away, did he move away?

Mum

No John moved in with his other woman.

Interviewer

Was that local, around here?

Mum

No and he lived 10 minutes away in G.

Interviewer

So what was your life like? You had three kids.

Mum

Looking back now it wasn't a life, I was just existing really. Thinking about it now, looking back, I never used to go out anywhere or anything like that, I just always had the kids. He went out that was it.

Interviewer

Was Chip going to school? What was Bill doing at this time?

Mum

Bill was in school, they were going to school. I didn't start having problems with Chip until the primary, the end of the primary school.

Bill he did have a view, like he wouldn't go to school at first but then his dad had him, his dad had him for twelve months and then Bill kept asking me to like come back home, he didn't like living with his dad. So he ended up coming back home and, touch wood, I've had no problems with Bill since.

Interviewer

OK, so let's now focus on Chip. When did the problems start with Chip?

Mum

The end of the primary school.

Interviewer

Just talk me through what happened.

Mum

I used to always be at the school. They used to say his behaviour, he was abusive towards the staff, with other kids and that. They excluded him in his last year and it's just been getting worse and worse.

Interviewer

So what happened during the permanent exclusion? Where did he go?

Mum

Nowhere, because it was coming up to the six weeks' holiday. He was due to start high school so he never went anywhere.

Interviewer

He started high school?

Mum

Yes, he started high school and I said to him just put everything in the past now what happened in primary school, make a fresh start. The first few weeks, I can only say weeks, he was OK, then I started having phone calls, his behaviour again, and they put him in the Learning Support Unit like isolation and nothing seemed to work with him. It was just gradually getting worse till he ended up at MEA [Mentoring for Educational Achievement] and then here at the PRU and that's it.

Interviewer

What about when we first met, you had a threat of eviction. What was going on that lead to that threat?

Mum

Chip's behaviour, he was smashing windows, him and Bill. That was an accident the wall on the front, they were messing about, the bricks must have already been loose and the wall came down. Then Chip used to climb up on the roof throwing bricks, climbing out of the windows, he was abusive to the neighbours, so I was reported to the landlord and they said they wanted me out but that's all sorted now.

The last few days, I don't know he seems different, he has been quiet.

Interviewer

And what do you think that is?

Mum

I haven't got a clue, you know your own kid and I think there is something wrong I just don't know what. The last few days he's been, I don't know, really quiet and that's unusual for Chip.

Interviewer

Various other things have changed since he was put on the Child Protection Register, in particular he is now coming here and when you are here he's attending and working quite hard. Have there been any other changes since that time?

Mum

Two weeks ago, I don't know whether the head of the PRU told you, I went out, they were all OK, my niece came down and was looking after them and Chip got drunk, I had half a bottle of brandy in the house, he got drunk and he wanted to kill himself. This was only two weeks ago. My eldest actually had to run out and drag him back in, he wanted to throw himself off the bridge or run in front of a car. They said he was crying but when I went back home, I was only out about an hour, as soon as I went in he says 'say summat and I'll hit ya'. I said 'Chip – go to sleep'. I don't know what started that off, I haven't got a clue. There was another incident, on Saturday over a mobile phone, my daughter has got a phone. Well at that time she was on the phone to her dad and her dad says no, learn to control him. I said it was to save any argument all I want John to do is to let Chip use his sister's phone tonight so I can get in touch with him, she can have the phone back in the morning. He started being abusive on the other end of the phone, this was telling Chip, that's alright then cos you ain't coming to live with me and he was going to get somebody to come down and sort Chip out but then that made Chip kick off even more, so yeah Chip was then being abusive back to his dad on the phone but then I couldn't blame Chip for that, I say when he's in the wrong but then I do say when I think he is in the right. There was no need for his dad to turn round and say he was going to get an adult down to sort him out. Chip has been really quiet since then. Chip and Tanya are really looking forward to going to live with their dad but after Saturday, I don't know whether it's got something to do with that, because then Chip said, all along Chip was saying he wanted to go and live with him but then after Saturday he says I ain't bothered anyway, I don't want to go and live with him anyway, but I know he did and he still does. Ever since then he has been quiet.

Now this morning we were waiting for the bus, all morning he was going to come in school, he saw these two kids about 16 or 17, he was talking to them, I said come on Chip because of the bus, he said no I'm not coming today, my exact words to Chip was – no they look like bag heads, you're not going with them, they look like druggies. He says I am, I said well that's all right then, you go with them I'm still attending the PRU and I'll notify the PRU when I get there to get the attendance officer on to you, and he came back and I said so you've made your mind up then and he never answered but he ended up coming with me today. I know if he had have gone with them they were the wrong ones, I know you can't judge people but they looked the wrong ones for Chip to be mixing with and I do wish his dad hadn't have said what he did on Saturday, but I did tell John, I said that's OK because the next meeting in two week time I am bringing all this up, I said you abused me because you had the drink in you again, I said and then you are telling your own kid you're going to get somebody down to sort him out and tell him that he's not coming to live with you, all over a mobile phone.

Chip has been different since Saturday. I was saying to my sister yesterday I know there is something wrong, I said I don't know whether it's got something to do with what John said to him on Saturday but what worries me now is, John is not here to sort him out, it's what I was trying to say in the meeting it's me that left to deal with it because now I have to be more careful knowing what he's threatened he's going to do only two weeks ago, and if he thinks he's not going to live with his dad, I don't know what's going on in his mind. I know these last few days he has been, I can't put my finger on it but he's been different. For one he hasn't been so clingy to me these last few days and that's unusual but he did hear me tell his dad you've got no right saying that to your own kid. See I don't usually stick up for Chip because most of the time Chip is in the wrong but Saturday he wasn't. He wanted the phone just so I could get in touch with him when I was out but his dad said no, he said it's his sister's phone. I said well to save any arguments all I want is for his sister to let him use the phone so I can get in touch with him and she can have the phone back in the morning, but since then he has been different.

Interview 2 PP – Parent Partnership Service

Interviewer

PP just tell me about your involvement with the family, maybe your involvement with mum, your involvement with Chip, just the story so far.

PP

Mum was referred to me in the summer from the PRU, the head of unit recommended that mum contacted us for support initially with having help to request a Statutory Assessment of Chip's SEN primarily because the support that the PRU were able to offer Chip was limited in the sense that they hadn't got the staffing, that he was having to have 2:1 staffing levels and they were finding it very difficult to manage his behaviour and it was quite apparent that he'd some significant behavioural, emotional and social needs. So mum made contact with me, I met her in the office in the summer and we went through what the Statutory Assessment process was going to be. I helped mum draft a letter to make that request to the SEN

Team and she hand delivered it but for some reason it wasn't received and things became a little bit messy so we had to pick things up again later on in September.

I kept involved with mum because it was apparent that mum had got some needs herself and I remember the first meeting one of the first things that she sort of laid on the table was 'I've had a letter today to say that I'm going to be evicted', so that actual interview itself, even though the reason she was with me was to get the Statutory Assessment, her mind was elsewhere. So we did what we needed to do and I explained to her well, let's just get this out of the way then this is one thing we can actually do something about today and then I went through, as far as my knowledge goes, what her options were about her housing and I made contact with Social Services for her at that stage, well she was going to ring the Family Solutions Team because she said that they'd already been involved with her. So that was my first encounter with mum, she was like, this is what she'd come for and then like there you go this is all the other stuff that I'm having to deal with.

One thing that struck me was that she'd bought a friend with her this friend was a very young girl in her late teens/early twenties and I remember thinking that it was (and she actually introduced her, this is my friend, I can't remember what the girl's name was and she sat in with us) but thinking that relationship, there was a very big age gap, and I don't know I kind of thought that that was quite an interesting dynamic really, just something I observed and I've not had any contact and don't know who this girl was but I just thought that it was quite interesting that mum classed somebody who was very much younger than herself as her friend on that basis and she'd come with her to support her at this meeting, so it was a bit odd.

Interviewer

Do you know who she was?

PP

No because that discussion then got took over with her stresses and mum was clearly distressed and anxious about the housing situation and all of the other stuff we just concentrated on that and then just got on with doing the letter and I said well this is one thing you can do, but I can't even remember the girl's name, she just introduced her as a friend, so that was quite an interesting thing I observed. So then my involvement was continuing to try and make sure that this Statutory Assessment process was going to begin and keeping on top of things really with mum and following things up and phoning, giving her regular phone contact and then linking in with what the head of centre was doing and had like a tag-team kind of approach.

Mum's often quite difficult to get hold of because she's got problems obviously, with putting credit on her phone. I'm not sure if sometimes that's a way of her staying quite elusive and her actually having a little bit of control in a situation and obviously I do believe that there are genuine reasons there as well that she hasn't got that much money to be able to keep on phoning people up, so I volunteered to do a little bit of that for her although my role is to try and empower her so she can do it. I know that if I don't take a bit more of a priority for her things won't get done and won't get followed up. I think quite a lot of my involvement has been giving her emotional support as well and just talking things through although I still feel I am only just touching the surface because there's a limit to how much detail you can go into and how personal you can get when that's not your primary role and your remit. I don't have anything to do with Chip I've only spoken to him a couple of times on the phone when he's answered the phone and he's always passed on messages to his mum.

Most of the work is with mum and trying to glean information from her and trying to give her that support. She didn't want to come to the last meeting and when I phoned up the day before and she said 'I'm not feeling very well' I thought well I'm going to press this because I know that's not why you've not come in but she just wanted to avoid that situation again. And you know she did say, ' Well I don't see what the point is'. And whether that's because she feels let down by the system or whether that's because she wants the system to fix something that she feels that she can't, but the system itself can't fix her, can't fix Chip, can support her to do it. But I am concerned really that she's kind of losing energy and losing strength to keep on seeing the battles fought, and that's just from my observations because I'm not as actively and intimately involved in the family as a family support worker would be for example, I'm not going to do home visits unless mum just can't get into the office most of it is over the phone and general support and probing a little bit and guiding her and getting her to do what she needs to do to show commitment to try and make things happen.

Interviewer

What are your ideas about, your hypothesis about this family? What do you think goes on?

PP

I think mum's very broken, I think the previous relationship has damaged her self-esteem quite a lot. I think that historically maybe there have been difficulties within the wider family and the family dynamics that she hasn't got the support network that she needs. I think she's blaming Chip quite a lot for his behaviour and some of that might be displaced because she knows that ultimately she's the parent in this situation and she hasn't got the power to fix it, she doesn't know what to do, so I thinks she's perhaps displacing some of her own issues about herself onto Chip. I think that Chip is desperately crying out for attention. I think that it's a mess that mum doesn't feel that she has any control in trying to resolve and trying to sort out, and that Chip is probably being blamed for the housing situation. If the other two siblings don't cause as many problems and he's the middle child then he's going to feel like he sticks out anyway and she's going to say well your brother's not like this, or your sister's not like this and I just think she's lost control. And I think she wishes that somebody could just wave a magic wand and sort it all out.

Interviewer

From your perspective, what would 'better' look like? What would be a realistic – let's start with a miracle question – what would be 'brilliant'?

PP

If she woke up tomorrow and the miracle had happened? The miracle question would be that Chip would get up on time, get himself dressed, that they'd have a normal family breakfast routine, that he would look forward to going to school, that he'd have a school not a PRU, that he'd be settled, he'd be achieving, he'd have the support that he needs, that she'd got routine, that she's got financial stability, that maybe she'd got a relationship in her life that was stable, that she'd got employment possibly, that they were a normal, as normal can be, functioning family.

Interviewer

And what do you think is realistic?

PP

I think it's realistic for Chip to be engaged in some kind of meaningful activities and I think it's realistic for mum to expect to have some support with her parenting skills and maybe some support with debt management and housing. I think that's the least because without those fundamental things anything else that's tried, anybody becoming Chip's friend or talking to him is just going to be a waste of time because there's no substance to it. They need stability.

Interviewer

What's your understanding of the housing situation now?

PP

I think that the eviction is being put on hold, my understanding, so there is a bit of stability there. Long term I don't know what's going to happen because my conversations with her have for the last couple of weeks primarily been about the meetings that have been taking place and trying to get the support from Social Services. My last conversation was after the last meeting that we had that took place, you know I encouraged her and I said that it was a positive meeting that key people were there, that the social worker had come and that the advice again was for Social Services to look at doing a core assessment of his needs and that she'd gone away to discuss it with her manager. But that we were all saying the same thing and left it at that really.

Interview 3 – FSW Intensive Family Support Worker (part of the Youth Offending Team)

Interviewer

FSW, first of all I'd like you to tell me what encounters you've had with Chip and basically what came out of these?

FSW

I've had a couple of sessions with Chip and his family, I've got to say that it's the early stages of assessment and like initial visits so I've probably had about two or three meetings with the family as a whole.

The first session I had was the assessment and when I went to do the visit, the mother was saying to me that she was really at her wit's end, she didn't actually know what she should do for Chip, what she shouldn't do for Chip. All she could see was that Chip was very obstructive at home, his behaviour was causing a lot of problems. The family were actually in the process of being evicted because of damage that had been caused in the house by Chip. We proceeded to do the assessment and we accepted the referral. One of the ideas that we had was that we'd actually do the meetings in the family home, so we tried to actually do that and the problem I was having was every time I went to do the visit Chip wasn't there. A lot of the time mum wasn't there either, which led us to believe that the mother's staying somewhere else.

The second visit was more of a crisis intervention. I had planned to go out but the mum actually phoned me and said 'Look I'm really struggling here, we've had a terrible weekend, a terrible morning' and it does tend to be on that basis when there's a crisis she will actually phone us rather than us being able to actually do the planned work that we want to do with the family to stop these crises in the first place. So the second time, this was the main visit, that was most revealing really. I went along and it was quite obvious that the mother was highly stressed. I could tell that she's actually been crying and I said, you know 'What's actually started it up?'

and she said 'Well, like normal I can't get Chip to go to school' she said that Chip had been sleeping on her bedroom floor. A key thing that I went away with in my own mind was the message that was coming across was that Chip is very clingy and she repeated herself a number of times and said 'I can't get away from him, I can't get a break from him, he's round my feet all the time'.

Chip's mother by her own admission, doesn't show a lot of affection at all. She said 'That's something I just don't do, it's not in my makeup', I said 'How do you actually show affection in any degree?' and she said, 'Well sometimes I'll play fight with him, but that will be it, but I've never shown him any sort of love, put my arms around him, show affection like that.' Chip was quite irate on that day when I went and it was difficult at first to try and actually get Chip to engage in the conversation because he just sat there really with a frown on his face which is not unusual for Chip because a lot of the times when I've seen him he does appear to be a very unhappy little boy. So I spoke to the mother about what had been going on and she said, something's got to be done, if he doesn't go to school and he's not going to behave I want him put in care. That's also been repeated a number of times, that she feels that she can't cope.

When I did the original assessment, she said 'Isn't there any way that I could have a break from him, that he could maybe go to a foster placement', or something like that, I presume that's what she was meaning. Family Solutions were involved which is the arm of Social Services. I don't think a lot of intervention work had actually been done with the family and before I knew it, the next time I actually contacted Social Services, they said that they'd closed the case. I went through the things that were bothering the mother first and it came out that it was behaviour and what she was actually meaning by his behaviour is that he does actually smash things up, like he'll break things, that he storms around the house, shouting at his mother.

While I was actually there he picked up a pool cue and he pointed it straight at his mother. I was sitting on the settee, she was sitting there and he was standing there. And anyway, I gently lowered the pool cue and he said, 'Don't touch that.' Anyway he did of his own accord, he removed it, and she said this was typical of what goes on here. After that, Chip seemed to calm down a bit, he was talking a bit more openly and I asked him 'What's making you so upset, do you feel that your mother doesn't love you?' (Mother was out of the room). He said that he did, that's what he believed and I said 'Do you think you're wanted at home?' and he said 'no' and I said 'Can you see the situation from where your mother's standing, how she feels?' He never answered that question. I said 'Do you ever smile much Chip?' and he said 'No' and just sat there with a frown on his face. Anyway I said 'Can't we have even a little smile out of you, even a tiny, tiny, tiny one?' and anyway he did and at that stage he was full of laughter, it was like I was actually looking at a totally different person. I tried to persuade him, because obviously one issue was that he won't allow CAMHS to actually do the assessment with him, and I said 'Why's that? Why don't you want to go and speak to these people?' and he said something along the lines of they think something's wrong with my head, and I said 'Maybe they just want to look at your feelings, the way you are, the way you are with other people, and just really to see if there's anything that they can suggest that may help. Because as you know there are a lot of people trying to help you – there's myself, your teachers at the PRU', and I also mentioned yourself as well. I said that all we're trying to do is not about putting you down, Chip, because I think that had happened quite a lot at home, a lot of negative comments because of the way he behaves, and I said really we're out for your good, in simple terms, I said we want to try and find a way that we can help you live a more happy life and get more out of life for yourself. Anyway he said 'Okay, I'll go along to CAMHS and I will go with you. ' I said OK.

Then his mother re-entered the room and I told her Chip's a bit more calm now, let's try to talk through what the difficulties have been. One of the key things was she wanted him to go to school, so at that stage he said he would go, I mean he has made statements like that before, but he does retract on these statements, saying he's going to do one thing, then when it actually comes to the time, he doesn't want to do it. Then he got upset again and said, 'I'm going to go and live with my dad' and mum said 'I've heard that all weekend, this is all he keeps saying.'

I was talking to Chip generally, and the mother was getting on her mobile phone, I wasn't aware at that stage who she was actually ringing, and she did actually phone the dad, and she actually put the phone on speaker phone and I heard her ask the dad 'I can't have him anymore, I don't want him, he wants to come and stay with you, will you have him?' and I heard him quite clearly say 'No, you'd better hand him over to Social Services, he's not coming here because of the way he behaves.' The call was ended then. Chip at that point burst into tears, I think that was quite a big thing for a boy of his age to actually have to hear, so I did what I could to comfort him, it was quite clear that his mother doesn't react to his emotions at all, the only comment she did make was 'You must think I'm awful.' I didn't answer, but she said I had to do that so that Chip would understand that his dad doesn't want him.

When Chip had calmed down a bit, I said 'Chip, what everybody sees is your be-haviour, they don't really see any further than that, they don't really see who you are, it's an obstacle with people. Now if we can work with you to change your be-haviour, maybe we can have a word with your dad and say, look we've done some work with Chip would you give him another chance, maybe come down for the weekend, or to spend the day, just to see how you get on.' Chip was quite excited about this and he said 'Yes I will work with you' so after that I did attend the PRU on two occasions, two different weeks, the first time, he was actually being taught, well they were trying to teach him and it was in a room on his own with one other member of staff and it was quite clear they were having difficulty actually keeping him there and this is a thing that happens as a regular occurrence from what I understand. He was refusing to do his work, anyway the teacher said 'Shall I leave you for a bit?' and I said 'Yes leave us for a bit' and I said 'What's the matter Chip, what's going on?' He said 'I don't want to be here I want to be at home, my mum's doing some decorating I want to go and help her. ' I said 'But you're only here for a couple of hours, it's not long, what work have you got to do?' Anyway I actually did the work with him, but the sort of way I try to interact with Chip is in a calm way, and to talk to him about things and make suggestions that may make him engage more and it does work on the whole when he's there, but the second visit I had, he wasn't there I think he was in the school about ten minutes. He came and wanted to go home and he did, obviously the PRU are saying we can't hold him here against his will, if he doesn't want to say, we've tried our best but it's just not working, so he went home. The mum, what we tried to do for her, was we wanted her to attend some parenting classes.

Last week I phoned her and I said, really we deliver a programme that is particularly geared to parents who have very difficult teenagers like Chip, and I said, you know, we do a lot of work around communication, around feelings things like that, it's not for little babies it is specifically for people of Chip's age. She said 'Oh yes, I want that' and the PRU had told me that she had wanted this before, so I gave her the time and explained where it was and she said she knew where it was and I sent her a leaflet so that she knew about the programme and where to go. She didn't actually attend.

So that was Monday, no attendance with Chip because he wasn't at the PRU so I couldn't do any work with him, she hadn't attended on the Tuesday, so there was no work done again, and it's just disappointing where we can actually go with this. I think Chip needs some sort of security in his life, these are the conclusions I've made. He needs some sort of security and he needs somebody who's got the time to sit down with him and to talk to him about his feelings and what's going on in his life and really to try and get him to open up how he feels about this type of thing, but I think this needs to be way from the normal distractions because a lot of the time he's wanting to go home, that's a key thing. The house isn't really suitable for doing this type of work in.

I don't know what the answer is, originally my plan was to go and pick him up from the PRU to bring him down to the Youth Offending Team to actually do some work with him and I was actually looking at doing some personal development work also doing some anger management actually that reminds me he did actually attend one of our sessions because I was told that he wasn't suitable for group work and when I spoke to Chip about this I said we've got this programme, it's only about you learning to respond to feelings and understand them a bit better and he came along and it's 5.15 on a Thursday night and he came along.

I hardly recognised him because he had his hood on and his coat and he didn't take his hood off and we all tried to engage him. Obviously the other teenagers that were there they sort of thought he was being offensive and not wanting to take part, to talk to people and another thing that I noticed when we were talking about something he'd make comments about what was being said and when you asked him again 'What did you actually say there Chip?' he wouldn't repeat it, he said nothing. It's quite clear that things that we were actually talking about were provoking some type of thought that he just came out with as if he'd thought it but not actually meant to say it.

A couple of times I thought I'd misheard and then after the session the other worker and I were taking a session and she said, 'No, I did hear him, you didn't misunderstand, he did, but he wouldn't actually...' and then he started saying 'How long have I got to stay?' and I said 'Well I did tell you it was til 7.15' 'Have I got to stay?' 'Well I can't hold you here, I'd like you to stay, you can get to know some of the other lads who are here, they enjoy coming here, maybe you will as well if you give it a chance' He said 'No, no I want to go' I said 'Well, you can go, we'll let you out if you want to go home, we can't hold you here.'

So that was another thing that we tried to do and I did speak to him about that afterwards when I visited him and I said 'Don't you want to attend the group sessions now?' and he at first was saying no, then we started talking about the way he's taught and I said would you prefer to work on a one-to-one basis? 'I don't like one-to-one, I hate that at the PRU.' I said 'So what would you actually prefer?' He said 'I want to be taught with other kids' I said 'Like the group that was here? But you didn't want to stay did you?' He said 'No, but I don't like work being done on a one-to-one basis with me' I said 'Well you're very welcome if you do want to start re-attending the group work sessions, if that's what you want to do, we'll meet that need for you.' He didn't attend afterwards, and that's it in a nutshell really.

Interviewer
Let's move on to the second part, what are your theories about him?

FSW

His mother wonders whether he's got ADHD, that's a label that she used quite a lot, and quite a lot of the kids when I do an assessment we usually find out that they're awaiting an assessment for ADHD. I don't know. I do think a lot of his problems stem from his dad not being there and I think that is really a major issue because when I said previously that he cried, he cried his eyes out. That boy was devastated, he was absolutely devastated, like it did quite upset me as well, and I thought I wished you'd told me what you were going to do, so I would have stepped in. So I think you've got the issue with his dad, I think you've got the issue with the mother, I do feel that he does feel unloved, that he's unwanted, that he's an obstacle, I think what he tries to do I think, because he's pushed away, I think that makes him more clingy. I was really surprised when his mother told me, I said why does he sleep on the floor, she said he doesn't say why, but I just can't get him out of the bedroom, he'll sleep on the floor and I thought crikey, it's like a dog would sleep on his master's bedroom floor, sort of thing, and I come away very often thinking that boy, all he wants is some love and I think this is where it's all gone wrong.

I think there are risks to him as he's developing as well because I had heard that he'd been hanging around with some older men, and thinking about, I mean there's never been any suggestion that there is any sexualised behaviour with Chip, but with a boy like Chip who's wandering around, who I don't suppose really, his mother would complain about him coming in late, and if he did meet men who were that way inclined, that he thought he was being shown love, I think that is a risk to him. When his mother told me that I said 'What do you think the reason is?' and she said 'Well I asked him and he denied it, but somebody saw him, I know for a fact.' I said 'Do you think that the motive is sexual?' she said 'I don't know' and I said 'Do you think it could be around drugs?' because he has been involved with drugs, although he won't admit it, this is all based on what the mother is actually telling us, and I said, 'You know it could be that'.

There are a few question marks. I think when he is going around, dossing around really, that's what he does in the evening, I think he is questioning what he's actually getting up to and he was actually seen. He had a friend at school as well and there was an incident, he broke into their house, there was some sort of argument about this lad's bike and I think he reported that it belonged to him and he actually broke into the house, so he's lost that friend now, so I don't think that he's actually got any friends at all now. I think mainly it is his mother.

The last time I actually visited Chip which was last Monday, obviously as I said previously he wasn't there, I had a word with the Deputy Head of the school and I was actually describing this situation, what happened at home and the way Chip actually sleeps on his mother's floor. She actually said, well maybe we're looking at all this wrong because they'd actually previously just told me that they were looking at some type of residential specialist placement for Chip for his needs, because they say we're not currently meeting his needs because we can't get him to stay so we can't deliver the work. She said maybe I should have a word with the Head about maybe trying teaching him at home, and anyway I said yes because

a) you may get him to relax because his mother will be around and he's in his own environment and

b) if the same teacher who's going in, then that may work because he may build a relationship up with that person because you haven't got the fear, is it a fear, when he's away from his mother, does he think his mother's going to run off? We don't really know what else is going on at the home. The Head certainly suggested to me that she wasn't convinced that she lives there all the time. I know that the older son is away at the moment, and I have made a couple of visits there where I've had excuses that I would question, but obviously I can't prove anything, you know, why she wasn't there. So I think maybe that could be one thing that could be looked at so at least Chip would be getting some type of education, and he may flourish in that type of environment.

Interview 4 – the SENCo from the excluding school

Interviewer

SENCo, we are talking about Chip and what I am trying to capture here is what was the secondary school experience for Chip when he was here.

SENCo

OK. I didn't have an awful lot to do with Chip but I am aware that obviously he was on the special needs register, he came to us in the September on the back of an exclusion from primary, I think had he been staying at primary he could well have been facing a permanent but because it was a transfer he came to us and there were problems right from the start. He was refusing to cooperate and aggression, threats to others and it escalated. He only did the first term in mainstream and after that he had a place in the Learning Support Centre.

Interviewer

What was your take on it, what do you think was behind it?

SENCo

I don't know, anger management, certainly he had huge issues we felt he was hanging about with the wrong crowd whilst he was out of school and that was having a huge influence on his behaviour in school and at home. We were aware there was no male role model for instance, no dad around and that, we think, he came and went to suit himself, he wrote his own agenda and he wrote his own agenda from a very young age and mum quickly ran out of ideas on how to cope so that basically he was writing his own agenda at home and he thought he could write his own agenda at school and to a degree he was dictating this.

Interviewer

Was he ever aggressive?

SENCo

Here? Oh yes, it was one incident after another with him with aggression and he could be very, very intimidating. It's a funny one really because I always thought whenever he came up against me that he was aggressive and I stood my ground and he backed off, and I always felt somewhere at the back of my mind I had the impression he was actually more in control than he appeared, but there was an element of it was deliberate, it may well have been genuine anger but some of it he pushed it further and tried to intimidate people, yes tried to intimidate people he appeared even more aggressive and when you actually faced him out with it, in my case, he backed off. I don't think he liked that.

Interviewer

Can I show you a picture (see figure 4.1) he has drawn of his time here in secondary school? – I asked Chip to draw me something that he remembers about secondary school, this is a picture that he drew. That's Chip and basically he is fighting Ian and what he was describing was all of Ian's friends around.

SENCo

There was an ongoing feud between the two families.

Interviewer

Can you remember any of that, how it arose here?

SENCo

No, I think they came with it, certainly quite early on we made moves to make sure they weren't in the same teaching sets because there were obviously problems right from the word go between the two of them.

Figure 4.1

Interviewer

When he talked to me I asked him about fights in junior school, because you are right he was facing permanent exclusion, and he said quite openly that he did start the fights. Is that the way it appeared here?

SENCo

He was definitely the aggressor, within a classroom situation he came across as very menacing towards others and if he had a downer on somebody like Ian he would keep going back for more.

Interviewer

Did he relate to anybody here? Was there anybody special that he took to?

SENCo

I don't think that he related to anybody, he *may* have related to YB, (then manager of LSC) obviously she was the one he spent most of his time with. In Year 7 he spent two terms in the LSC and then we attempted this stage reintegration the following year. The continuity would have been YB so he may have related to her but I doubt it. Yeah, I would say he didn't relate to anybody because the only one I would imagine who stood a chance of making a relationship with him was Y [manager of the learning support unit] if she didn't manage it, no would be the answer, to my knowledge anyway.

Interviewer

Is there anything else that sticks out in terms of your memory of Chip here?

SENCo

Well only that he was extremely difficult from the word go, difficult to engage, if you went to have a conversation with him you would struggle to have a conversation with him because, from our point of view I just felt he didn't like me and I have had very little to do with him. It's difficult to form a relationship with kiddies when you only see them in passing. Because obviously I was around, I was in the area I would pop in and out because there were times when an incident had blown and I was there as part of the management process of it but you couldn't engage with him you couldn't have a conversation with him. He would struggle to look at you, he would avoid looking at you if he could, he wouldn't meet your gaze and he wouldn't want to engage so basically if you made any overtures you were effectively rebuffed, you go nowhere with him. You got very little, you got a blank basically.

At one stage I think mum was hoping for a diagnosis of ADHD, we in school did not feel he filled any of the criteria, we didn't get as far as CAMHS but we didn't feel he was ADHD, I still feel there was a huge element of calculation in his behaviour, that for some reason, maybe in his past, he had built up a shell, he was angry he had something there he was trying to contain perhaps, I don't know I'm not a psychologist. Well I can only speculate like everybody else. I don't know maybe his parents had split up at a very early age and perhaps he felt rejected, maybe there had been some abuse in the background somewhere I don't know, but certainly I would say something in his early life turned this child into what he was by the time we got him because he was already well formed by then. Something had gone wrong.

Interview 5 – The second within school exclusion manager's story

Manager

Well first of all he is a lovely kid so it was a great shame when we came to the end of what it is that we could do with him. I felt most of the time that Chip chose the way he behaved, he had a number of family circumstances that you could never get to the bottom of particularly. I felt the absence of his dad was a big, big thing in Chip's life but before he did leave he had seen his dad a couple of times so I hoped that things would get better from that. When Chip went off on one of his moods he was aggressive, he was arrogant, angry, there was just absolutely no reason for being, absolutely. There were circumstances within the family that I felt weren't right. There was a lot of negative from mum and I understand some of it because, you know, she is on her own she is fed up and she just wants her kid to be OK in school and leave her be, but there were a couple of times when I know he has been left at home on his own, when they had gone to Blackpool, there was the occasion where he had burgled his cousin's house. You know things that aren't normal, whether that was attention seeking behaviour in the end I don't know.

His dress was absolutely appalling most of the time, we must have given that kid two school jumpers, ties every week you know just to try and make him feel part of the setting that we were. I don't think it helped Chip particularly when I came in and changed the environment. It's a personal thing but I felt it operated as a youth club before I was here and that is not what I wanted as an inclusion centre for secondary school, so I did change things and it was hard for Chip to get that message because he had previously been held onto by dictating what he was prepared to do and being allowed to do that. Obviously I am a very different person and that wasn't going to be the case and I needed to move Chip forward. Whether the pace was too quick I don't know but in the end there was very little I had got left for him.

Interviewer

You mentioned when he had got one on him – if you could bring to mind either a day or a morning or an incident when you knew he had got one on him, just talk me through actually what happened.

Manager

Just before we broke up for Christmas, the last day of term, I thought we are going to have a fantastic day today. I had bought them all a Christmas present in, we had chocolate, sweets, cake, pop, it was all Christmas party spirit, it was lovely. At the time he was with CS and he was also with a young lady called Jo, who we have still got in school. Jo suffers quite severe speech problems and it was the in thing at the time to call her 'fish face'. Jo to be fair takes a lot of stick before she explodes. One of the LSAs [learning support assistants], was in there sitting with Jo, they were doing Christmas posters and stuff and Chip just came out with an absolute barrage of insults at Jo. Every word that you can possibly think of, fucking fish face, fucking bastard, the lot, so in the end he absolutely lost his temper at this kid, the tears were trickling down on the poster, he stood up to go and get both of them to bring them in to me and he ran, Chip absolutely fled because he could see the anger that he had caused, five minutes later he came strolling into my office 'If he'd touched me I was gonna kill him' you know the usual.

When I spoke to Chip he couldn't comprehend that he had possibly upset this girl because it's normal, it's normal to land the barrage of insults that she had received and I witnessed that when I had his brother. I had his brother in isolation while he was in the Learning Support Centre and it was normal behaviour for Bill just to walk up to Chip and head butt him and Chip would just lose it. Bill knew he would lose it, so we'd spark constantly together. Yes, Chip's older brother. I worked tirelessly with Bill as well because of alternative curriculum, Bill was totally disaffected, he wasn't enjoying school, he didn't want to be here and I worked really hard to get him linked with a company to do painting and decorating, it's really hard on alternative curriculum to get painting and decorating because of the insurance and everything. I met with these blokes 7 o'clock in the morning, 6 o'clock at night when they could come in and we set it up and Bill lasted a fortnight tops. Because there's no stability at home, we don't have to do things, you know, we do as we please.

Interviewer

You are saying this was the last day of term, it was a Christmas event, he's been insulting this girl and the adult male in the room got basically mad with this, Chip ran off and eventually came back in saying 'if he'd have touched me I'd have killed him'.

Manager

Yes, total denial that he could have possibly hurt Jo because it's normal to land the barrage of insults that he landed.

Interviewer

What happened then, did he go home?

Manager

No I took him downstairs into the reception room which was then away from them, away from Jo, away from his audience really. It was half day luckily so they were going at lunch time, I mean there was about 15 minutes to the bell and I just said to him, 'you sit here, calm down and we will deal with this when you come back'. Exclusions don't work for Chip, not fixed term because it just gives him a licence to do what he wants to do out on the street.

Interviewer

I'd like to show you a picture that he has done for me of his life here – this is out the back, that's Chip, these are Ian's cousins or family and this is an occasion where he fought and Chip has said quite openly that he would initiate these fights. Can you remember this incident or incidents like it where he actually got involved in a fight with other pupils?

Manager

No he has never, ever been involved in a fight with another student while I have been about. I have never witnessed Chip fighting. I have witnessed him winding people up, I have witnessed his arrogance, I have witnessed him being nasty but I have never witnessed Chip put a finger on anybody.

Interviewer

Did Chip get involved with fights once he was here?

Manager

He may well have done because obviously he went last January and I had only been here since September so I had very little time with Chip to be fair. I mean, the way that division looks we had a lot of trouble with his brother Bill's year, with whites and Afro-Caribbeans against Asians and he is very, very racist, a very racist young man. I don't know whether that's because again, as he would with Jo, he would take the mick out of anybody who was not white.

I actually think it was a Friday when it went off but I remember one incident when the head teacher spoke to him and he was so rude to the head teacher, he really was rude and he just walked out and I don't know whether that was the fight, I can't remember so I don't know. I remember his mum coming in once and she sat (again I hadn't been at the centre long) and cried. She was absolutely desperate for help with Chip and we did our usual, refer to CAMHS and bring any support in that we can physically do and I always remember getting the letter again from CAMHS and apparently he refused to go.

Interview 6 – Staff from the Pupil Referral Unit

PRU teacher

Yesterday Chip came in and he was just really having a heart to heart basically and the gist of it, I think, stems back to dad, the anger inside him is to do with dad not wanting him so this 'I don't care' attitude is really because dad doesn't care and I think he takes it out on his mum, he blames his mum for the split up in some ways but other ways he doesn't. He told me that mum and dad had been separated four years ago. Dad, I believe, has gone to live in Yorkshire with a partner and the partner has got two children, one of whom is disabled. Dad looks after this disabled child and Chip's attitude was, quite rightly, 'well dad looks after her and feeds her and buys her stuff but he never did it for me. Why couldn't he do it for me when I was that age?' So I thought there's a lot of resentment building up. If mum had phoned dad the other day (yesterday) when the YOT worker (intensive support worker from the youth offending team) was on the phone to say could dad just have Chip for a few days just to give her a bit of a break, Chip and mum a bit of a break from each other, dad says 'no' if mum wants a break then mum should get in touch with Social Services. So basically he is denying any emotional responsibilities for Chip.

Chip says when, sometimes, when they see the dad, which is not very often, I think he says about three or four times this year, dad says when they go up there you can stay with us but it never takes place and then when dad is on the phone while Chip is at home dad says no. He is saying dad won't give him any money, dad won't give mum any money, I think he said he bought him a pair of new shoes at the beginning of Year 9 but I think mum is struggling, she's on benefits and not working and obviously now Chip is a teenager they all want things and it's expensive enough to run a home with food and that and mum has got Chip and two others to look after I think he is just hurting inside basically because he feels his dad does not want anything to do with him. He is getting to the point now, he said yesterday, that he is supposed to be going to dad's on his mum's birthday which is around Christmas time but Chip has decided in his own mind now that he wants to go out for a meal with his mum and spend time with his mum and try to support mum.

It is nice because I think what he thinks, Chip has blamed his mum and not particularly for the split up but what he is blaming her for now, she meets men and he says she cheats on them, and I said well probably. I suppose going with other men, but I said to Chip maybe your mum feels hurt as well and your dad cheated on her and he came out with 'I'll never cheat on anybody' and he basically admitted yesterday that he thinks a lot of his behaviour is because of his home and the split up and the way dad has been towards him I think he has sort of tried to get in his brain and understand dad doesn't care but as a child he can't accept that yet. A colleague came in as well and we had a little chat. She talked about personal circumstances and I tried to explain about my personal circumstances. We talked about him trying to get a job trying to get money and he said well he could get a job, but he needs to get a c.v. We said we probably could help him with that. He actually, I think, was crying out for a lot of help yesterday and telling me in my heart I felt Chip you're not a bad one, you know you are hurting inside and this pretence is a barrier, I don't care because he feels hurt. He spent till about 10 o'clock talking and he was quite happy to talk, he doesn't normally talk to any of us here but he said 'well I'm talking now aren't I?' but he wasn't prepared to do any work afterwards and I felt it was enough for him to get all that off his chest and we just let him go and he walked off calmly.

Now this morning, it's quite interesting, he came into school about 8.45 and normally we are sending him to the quiet room because we have got a few staff out again this morning, he wanted some toast and I said Chip how about you help to do the toast and he did, I got him to wash his hands and he made the toast and he has taken on quite a bit of responsibility, he has done that, no problems at all no showing off nothing and then of course this lady came in for the talk and he has gone down to that so I feel we did make sound headway, but what we can do to help him and mum now, I think, is try get him to have counselling and he said 'no'. Maybe he feels happy to talk to us but I think if we can work out something and he is keeping it calm at home with mum and not blaming mum so much and not shouting at one another then maybe he and his mum may be able to understand the situation with dad and in time Chip might be able to understand about his dad.

He is not a bad lad at all and he knows right from wrong and he does care a lot, I think he cares and loves his mum and he cares and loves his dad but he wants a lot of love back. We were talking about a pupil who has recently started since last half term, only been here about four weeks, quite a horrendous background and he was truanting from school, there were problems at school, he's been out of school for a long time, he's come here, he's been very polite, he's conformed with our Unit, the beat officer that comes in has said after the other day what has happened to Phil, because Phil hasn't been heard about in the community for the last two weeks, we told the officer he's in school, he's attending every day, he's taking part in all the activities here, there's no problems with his behaviour and he is doing really well, but a member of staff said the other day perhaps we should get him back into main-stream now that he is settling down and I said no because why should we do that at the moment if he is stable for once in his life, why push him back into an environment when he is stable in this school (and the community is stable from him) so why put him back into the system to fail again?

5

Jack

Jack is eleven years old. He is described by his mother as 'mixed race'. He is the youngest of five children. Jack was coping well with primary school until his behaviour there deteriorated following his witnessing of domestic violence and his father ignoring him following leaving the family home. A number of behaviour management strategies were attempted within school with limited success. It was decided that a 'managed move' to a Pupil Referral Unit (PRU) would offer Jack a more appropriate curriculum to meet his needs and enable him to get back on track before transition to secondary school.

Jack attended the Pupil Referral Unit for about a year. At the time of interview he was about to begin mainstream secondary school.

Interview 1 – Jack's mother

Interviewer
I just wondered if you could tell me a little more about him? Just what he's like?

Mother
Right. He's very caring, loving, but Jack's got a very insecure side which basically started his behaviour at school. Basically because he was witness to his dad's domestic violence but really bad. There was one case when the police and dogs had to come to the house and Jack's witnessed. All four of them were in fact. Jack was six at the time but he was found like hiding between the wall and the dryer. Like you know, so it was like since that day Jack completely changed personality. And basically it worked out where he was going to school he started to be naughty, then he started to work out in his own little head, if he was naughty then he would get sent home. So him getting sent home, he'd be able to check if I was okay.

93

Interviewer

So almost to check how you were really?

Mother

Yeah, he would do anything. Refusing to eat his dinner, not sitting on a chair, saying he wanted the toilet when he'd just been. And then when the teacher went to come over to him he'd like be sitting there saying 'you can't touch me' and go on the defence like that. And then the only thing that would calm him down was by phoning me so in the end he'd get what he wanted, exactly what he wanted. I offered, when he started to get really naughty, to sit in class. And I did actually just start a new job as well. At the time, but at the end of the day I had to say my family came first, and I couldn't, it was making me really nervous going to work anyway. And I had to keep leaving work and coming home to get him. Basically, Jack was excluded in the end, 'cos they actually said, they sat down and said 'we can't give Jack the help that we feel he needs'. And it was true.

Interviewer

What do you think they would say was the help that he needed? That they couldn't give?

Mother

Basically, they said, they had a mentor come in, right, but they went away, she was only allowed to be at the school twelve weeks, a twelve week course, which was what they were willing to pay for in the Education. Well, to supply and his twelve weeks was up. In that twelve weeks Jack's behaviour, the mentor actually spoke to me, she said, you know 'I don't think the school has given him nowhere enough support. I believe Jack is being accused of things he didn't even do.' And it's got to the stage where if he was accused of something he would just say 'yeah, yeah, it was me'. Because he said, in the end, his favourite word was, 'I can't be bothered anymore'. Because that's all he kept saying, it was true. But after the twelve weeks, they couldn't offer me any more help. So I contacted them, CAFCASS (Children and Family Court Advisory and Support Service), myself which were absolutely wicked. But in the end, what they were interested in was the access to seeing their dad. And I think ... what is it you do, sorry?

Interviewer

I'm a Clinical Psychologist.

Mother

Yeah. I think we had to see someone the same as you. They basically said, they had an interview with the boys and they said I offered a happy environment and they were best when their dad weren't around. It's best really and he never had any access at all granted. So there's not enough help in the school, they can't. Mentors should be on, in every school, because Jack goes to Spring-gate now and in that year Jack has blossomed and he's done a lot more in a year than he's done in three years at that school. Because all they tend to do is shout, send him out the class, send him home, send him home. That's their answer to everything and it just doesn't solve anything. And they're too quick to exclude them now, I believe.

Interviewer

It sounds from what you're saying that there wasn't a specific incident which led to him being excluded?

Mother

There was loads of incidents.

Interviewer

But there wasn't one where they said, 'right that's it'?

Mother

No, no. Because there was an incident with this little girl and they kept fighting. But they said because Jack is a boy and she is a girl, they made the issue Jack's and not her. But I even tried to explain, the little girl, the nasty things she was saying to Jack because it turned out her mum was going out with his dad. And she was saying 'oh, your dad took me to so and so last night. You never see him because he doesn't want to see you.' And she was saying nasty things like this to him so he was ripping up her work. And even when I explained what she was doing and in the end they separated them into different classes but it still didn't solve it. Then in the end it felt as if he was let down by the teachers himself and he just said, 'what is the point?'

Interviewer

Did he ever have any short-term exclusions?

Mother

It felt like he'd go to school on the Monday and on the Wednesday I'd be having a phone call to say 'leave him at home for the rest of the week' and I'd say 'it's three days'. I'd ask for work, but it's me that asked for work. And half the time you wouldn't get it so it was like he was having two days at school it felt like. Two and a half days. So, and that was over six months.

Interviewer

So it feels like the support for him dried up? How have things been for him since he's been at Spring-gate? Difficulties there with his behaviour?

Mother

A bit hard at first. But, I think he realised that having a little temper weren't going to get him sent home. So he thought 'Whoah, what can I do?' And I went into school, and I worked with school. I go in there odd days and if they go on trips then I go. And get on really well with all the kids there and Jack was like, you know, Jack knows. And I've got a male friend but he hasn't moved in, nothing like that. Jack sees him as a friend because that's what he is. He spoke to Jack and reassured Jack that nothing would ever happen to me while he's not around and he'll make sure that even though he's at work, he said 'I'll phone your mum and she's okay. And when she's at work she's trying to make your life better for when you've grown up'. And Jack, he's grown up a lot, a hell of a lot.

Interviewer

Reassuring him of your safety while he's away at school.

Mother

And his dad has completely stayed away. It's made a massive difference.

Interviewer

It's given him a chance to settle down.

Mother

He still goes on one when he bumps into his dad though. If he sees him he goes all insecure. And he uses the word hate. Which you know isn't allowed in the house. And he hates everyone and everything and he goes in his bedroom and says 'I don't want to live here anymore' but you know. I can't imagine what it's like for them having the old, thinking your dad don't want you. So that's Jack down to a 't'. He's got a heart of gold.

Interviewer

And he's told me he's moving schools to ...

Mother

Which he's absolutely excited. He's always, always wanted to go there and he thought he'd never go there because of going to the PRU. And you know Lodge Oak? He thought that's where he'd end up.

Interviewer

He'd automatically move there?

Mother

That's for the older kids. And he knows the kids that go there; they tend to end up in young offenders, or young baby fathers or young baby mothers. And he doesn't want to be like that so I think. His brother, his brother's just left and he's going to college doing air conditioning and refrigeration and he's like following...

Interviewer

Sort of looking up to his brother?

Mother

Yeah, and he looks up to Andrew as well. And Andrew's an IT teacher and he just said 'Jack, it starts at school'. I think it's important for boys to have male role models. You know some people say it isn't, it really is. I can only do so much.

Interviewer

It certainly sounds to me that Jack is looking forward to moving to .....

Mother

Definitely. He's already said to me that he's not going to get into trouble even if someone tries to have a fight with him. He said, 'I'm going to walk away mum and do all the things that they've taught me at Spring-gate. My stress ball' He said, 'I'll have it in my pocket'. And he said 'there's no way. I'm going to leave, get a good job, a nice car and big house'. And all this, so yeah.

Interviewer

He's got his aspirations? It sounds like his previous primary handled him quite differently to how Spring-gate do? What things are different? Why are things working at Spring-gate when they didn't at...?

Mother

I believe the teachers have got a hard time. You know, definitely. But I, they don't ... they tend to see the moment as it is at the time. They don't look into why that child is behaving like that. They don't really care, I don't think. As long as they're not disturbing that class they think. I know it is concerning. They're more bothered, not of Jack but of other parents complaining. That's what they were bothered about. And I said I understand, because if my son or daughter came home and kept saying – oh so and so was doing this – so and so – we couldn't do that today because ... But their answer was to throw him out the class all the time. Send him home. Send him home and in the end he was just doing two days a week.

Interviewer

How did he get on with the other pupils at Greenfield?

Mother

That's you know, that's my main concern because he was out of school for five months, Jack, because the paperwork got mixed up.

Interviewer

So he was out of school for five months?

Mother

Five months. So when I took him to. I think that had a big effect as well. When I took him and I appealed against it. I said, if you take his peers from around him then he feels as though everything has broke down in his life at the moment, with his dad and everything else. I said he's going to give up Jack. So he ended up having a place but it's like he had best friends and what Jack did. Jack was actually causing problems and sorting out them bullies but Jack was getting into arguments that didn't concern him. But he thought and he took it on his own head that's what he should do. And it was funny the situation that happened in the house. He didn't like people arguing and shouting but then it turned out it made him look a bully. But even then, I can remember a teacher saying to me, 'I felt like patting Jack on the back for what he did earlier, but I obviously couldn't condone the amount of violence or how aggressive he was', but it was directed at a bully which met his match.

Interviewer

So it sounded like he had some good relationships at Greenfield? With pupils. And you mentioned that he was out of school for five months, so how, that process? I guess he went to Spring-gate after those five months? What was he doing for those five months?

Mother

He was out of school for five months before he was allowed the place at Greenfield. He was supposed to start in September. You know, the new term. They said, 'There's a mix up in the paperwork'. I had to appeal against it. He was literally out of school for five months. And it weren't until I threatened the Education with private tuition, which could cost x amount a day, that all of a sudden there was a place. But until then it was me teaching him and I didn't know where to start. I was literally doing a bit of maths, a bit of English, reading, we did his writing, but I think he was sick of me. He was sick of the sight of me in the end!

Interviewer

It was difficult I guess not having the pupils and the onus on you all the time. That's tough. So he had a five month wait before he went to Spring-gate.

Mother

Then he started and everything was okay and then they kept saying he's being disruptive and then they got into the pattern of sending him home. And I did try to sit them down and tell them. I said, 'Ring me, I will come up and sit there'. They was like 'No, because it's like he's getting special treatment'. And I was trying to explain. I explained to them word for word what he was doing. I said 'he's really really in-secure at the moment'. I said, 'He's quite happy being at home with me 24/7 to know exactly what I'm doing, if I'm okay.' 'This is a nine year old boy', I said 'and it's quite sad to say that he thinks he should be at home protecting me.' They were good. I can't knock (head teacher). He was. He did try and support but they haven't got counsellors, mentors. They've got no connection. Even the mentor said it to me. She said, 'If I was there permanently they'd never have trouble'. They don't understand Jack. They haven't got a clue. Their answer is shouting, shouting, shouting and Jack hates shouting. He'd start saying, 'don't shout'. The teacher, a certain teacher, was like shouting and would say 'You can't muck about in my lesson' and he'd say 'but I haven't done anything'. And he said, 'What's the point? What's the point in be-having?' So....

Interviewer

So, it felt like when he was being okay, he was being blamed for things that weren't his fault?

Mother

That's what he said.

Interviewer

How are things with him now in Spring-gate? Friends? How's he getting on there?

Mother

He's, he has certain friends. He doesn't associate with them outside school. He's quite funny because he actually does say now, he comes home and says 'Okay mum' he says about a certain name and goes 'He's so naughty' and I'm like 'Jack, not so long ago you were a bit like that.' He goes 'Oh Mum, I can't believe I was that naughty'. He goes 'Seriously, I was like that?' And I'd go 'Yeah' and he'd say like 'Oh, I nearly got into a fight today' and I'd say 'Why?'. And he'd say, because one of his teachers is having a baby and he said someone had pushed her in the belly. And alarm bells start to ring in me at things like that. And he said 'I just went mad'. But they take him to the office and say 'Phone mum' and they know I'm going to talk to Jack for ages. And him like 'You've let yourself down Jack.' And he's like 'I know'. I said 'You don't want to come home do you? You don't want it to be like it was before?' I said do you want to go and he's calmed down. And you can hear his voice.

The teachers are amazing at the school. They really are. Every single teacher. Every single teacher is like a counsellor, mentor, a teacher, a friend. They're brilliant there. They really are. They don't get paid near enough, any of them. Because when the kids there want to have a little moment. And you never hear them shouting. They just take them to one side and like they talk to them, listen and it's all about that person at the time. Fantastic.

Interviewer

You say that Jack has blossomed this last year? How is he getting on academically?

Mother

Academically, in the last year, he liked drawing. He's joined a football team. He goes to coaching. He's been on three coaching courses. And he just gets on with every-one else. Now his social skills are brilliant. And he actually does talk about his dad now and without getting angry as he used to. And he like says at the end of the day it's his loss because he'll regret it when I'm older. And he's probably regretting it now. His temper, because it used to be from one to straight up. There was no in-be-tween, it was just so fast it was kind of scary and now it's like, he's had that many stress balls!

And like today, I'll give you a prime example, about three months ago he had one of his little tantrums at school, he threw a teacher's pen, then he found out it was the teacher that's now having a baby and he didn't realise that he broke it at the time. She told him 'You know you broke my pen Jack' and he was like really upset about this pen. And at the weekend he went and bought like a fluffy pen, a bird with wings and that. And he's took it to school today and he's really looking forward. All weekend he's been like, 'Don't let me forget it mum' and I'm like no, I won't. He's gone to school today and took it. He's like, 'She's shown me a picture of her scan today as well'. He was really looking forward to it. He looks forward to going to school.

Interviewer

Did he before?

Mother

No. He dreaded it. His head was bad, falling down.... He pretended that he fell outside off his bike and hurt his arm. This is the extent he went. So what I did, I said okay. I put a cold flannel on there. He was sitting on that chair and I said to him 'Oh gosh' about five minutes later. I went like this, put my arms up in the air, stretched them up and down and said 'I bet you can't do that. Ten tries really fast' I said, 'I'm kind of fit considering I don't go to the gym'. He went, 'No, that's easy' and he did it. I said to him ' I see your arm's alright then!' He went 'oh mum!!'

Interviewer

We were talking academically. He said to me how much he likes to be outside, all weathers really. Have you any concerns about when he goes to the new school?

Mother

Yes, because, I think my main concern is he's going to a school where there's a lot more kids than sixteen. I don't know if he'll feel a bit overwhelmed or what. There's no way he can't be feeling a bit frightened of it all. But I think you tend to feel like that when you start high school anyway. But, in another sense, I think the more people around the better Jack seems to be. And he's bumped into a few friends from primary school and they are going there as well.

Interviewer

Is that because of the way he's so social?

Mother

Yes. Because I think what it is, the people, like the weekend. There's five of them. They put all their money together and they bought a tent. They pitched up in the back garden and they slept, four Friday night and five Saturday night. They slept Friday, Saturday. They went to a fair and for a bike ride and Sunday they all went to bed at seven o'clock last Sunday. Jack said ' I think I'm coming down with something'. I said 'No Jack, you're just tired'. Jack's idea that was as well. So, it's things like that.

Interviewer

Will he have people he knows going up to ..... with him?

Mother

Yes. I've just found out that he knows quite a lot of people in the year above. Having an elder brother as well, he knows everybody. I think I'm more worried than he is. I haven't said anything to him. I just said like 'are you nervous?' He said, 'I can't wait. I can't wait.' Because so and so goes like, the one main person, I think he's going there. But I don't know.

Interviewer

It sounds like Jack has moved on a lot and how he might handle the situation. Big changes. Will he have an opportunity to go there for a couple of mornings?

Mother

This is something I've got to ask. I was talking to her on the phone today. I said, 'can I go there?' Because I haven't been to that school and speak to the teachers and that. And I said is it going to be like when you feel that the kids are ready to go back to mainstream school? They usually go with them for one day, a couple of days. I said, 'how's it going to be?' Is he just going to be thrown into the deep end? Because that does concern me. Because Jack sort of said that he wanted to be treated like everyone else starting the new school. I said 'don't you want anyone to go?' he said no because then they'll know what school I've come from. He said 'I'd just prefer going with everyone else'. No he said, 'I don't want to start getting the blame for things just because of the school I came from.'

Interviewer

What would be your hopes for Jack for the future?

Mother

Hopes. My hopes for Jack, obviously to be happy and healthy but to do the end of his education and leave. And basically not isolate himself. Mix with the other kids and get good grades and leave and get a good job. Yeah. That'd be it for me.

Interviewer

Would there be anything you'd change for pupils in the process of being excluded? From the benefit of your experience with Jack?

Mother

I would highly recommend if they came from a certain background, like domestic violence or something, because most of the problems do start in the home, and there is always something going on in the home which leads to their behaviour in school. I don't care what anyone says, for me it does. If they can get to that problem. I believe either mentor or counselling would be absolutely fantastic. If you can agree to a child having one or the other I think you're halfway there.

Interviewer

Something about understanding what's happening outside? Rather than like you were saying, straight in front of you?

Mother

There's always something behind a kid who's a bully or being bullied. There's something. There's always a story there. Definitely.

Interview 2 – Head of Pupil Referral Unit

Interviewer

If I could just perhaps ask you a little bit about maybe Jack to start with, a little bit about his background?

PRU Head

Jack came from Greenfield. He was displaying disruptive behaviour there, wouldn't co-operate with class teachers, would walk out of the room and maybe verbal regards staff, abusive, swearing. We went to a few meetings with the head teacher, before multi-agency meetings where he actually got support, fifteen hours that was the PAP (Pupil Allocation Panel) and the second meeting was for it still hadn't worked having support from the behaviour support team. We looked at a managed move as a fresh start for him so he came here. It has been just about a year. When he first started we did get a lot of verbal abuse off him. Just the same, displaying the same behaviour. With, it was hard work for the staff, circle time where he could talk, behaviour management. It took time to build up trust with the staff. It gradually improved, this term we've really noticed the difference, and he has matured and grown up.

He was one of the children who the Ofsted inspectors spoke to last week and even he noticed how mature he was compared with some of the others. His behaviour was excellent he had good manners. So it's twelve months but I think he has wanted to improve his behaviour. Before Christmas he didn't care, he still went, 'it doesn't matter what I behave like'. After Christmas I think he started to realise that the time was running out in our unit. He was going to go back to mainstream school from that point he said I don't want to be excluded from the key stage 3 school I don't want to go to the key stage 3 PRU. And he started to pull his behaviour up. He's one of the successes.

Interviewer

It sounds like he's turned himself around partly as he wanted a fresh start. What did you think it was that you thought he needed?

PRU Head

I think a lot of these things with Jack is emotional and I think he's witnessed domestic violence with mum and dad. Mum said dad sometimes sees him in the street and ignores him, drives past and that really upsets him. Sometimes on a Monday we know if he's actually seen his dad and ignored him because his behaviour is totally different from when he'd gone home on the Friday. His behaviour's really changed and so we know he saw Dad in the street. So emotionally, things to do with mum and dad, I think that was a lot of his problems.

Interviewer

It sounds like he'll be finishing in a couple of week's time. How do you think he'll get on now?

PRU Head

I actually think he'll do really well. He's already been to meet the special needs staff at Grove secondary. We went yesterday. He knows who the SEN teacher is, who are the support staff. They've been told if they need time out, if they feel that their work's getting too hard and they can go to the Unit to talk to staff, then they are allowed to do that. He has got his fifteen hours support to carry on when he goes. He's got it for another year and if he still needs it they will just reapply for continuation, as he'll still get those hours. They're going two days next week.

Interviewer

So he's getting transition ...

PRU Head

All the primary school children go for one day, but they are going for the two. So they can get to know the school and the staff. But they were introduced to the Head and they know the Head of Year. They know the SENCo and they know the support staff.

Interviewer

They've got lots of people to go to if they are worried.

PRU Head

Yes. The SENCos are very much like the staff here. Down to earth with the children so they are more or less like being in here. I know they've got more children but they have that security of a small base while they reintegrate.

Interview 3 – Jack

Interviewer

Have you got any brothers or sisters?

Jack

I've got three sisters and one brother. All older.

Interviewer

How old are you?

Jack

Eleven.

Interviewer

Are you going to a new secondary school soon?

Jack

Grove Secondary School.

Interviewer

What's it like having older brothers and sisters?

Jack

Alright. My older brother has just left but he's going back for his exams.

Interviewer

Was he at Grove?

Jack

And my sisters have left as well now. My brother is 14, no 15.

Interviewer

How old are your sisters?

Jack

One's 18, one 19 and one's 21.

Interviewer

So you're the youngest. What's that like?

Jack

It's alright.

Interviewer

When you're not at school, what do you like to do?

Jack

Ride, play football. All I do is mostly play football.

Interviewer

You like lots of things outside? Who do you play football with?

Jack

My cousin.

Interviewer

Family close by.

Jack

Just down the road. My mates.

Interviewer

Friends from school.

Jack

People that live around there.

Interviewer

Do you like music? What music do you like?

Jack

Yeah. Everything really.

Interviewer

What about TV, films?

Jack

Yeah.

Interviewer

Any favourites?

Jack

Not really cos most of the time I'm outside.

Interviewer

So you really like to be outside. Does that depend on the weather?

Jack

No. most of the time I do go out.

Interviewer

How do you know when it's time to go home? Does your mum tell you?

Jack

Depends on what day and where she is. Or if I've got school.

Interviewer

What are things like at Spring-gate?

Jack

It's good. I don't know really, just ...

Interviewer

What's good about it?

Jack

All the teachers are good and they help you a lot.

Interviewer

Teachers are helpful.

Jack

Yeah. They just learn you a lot really.

Interviewer

Is there a favourite thing you like to do here?

Jack

Probably maths.

Interviewer

Do you get much time to play football?

Jack

Yeah.

Interviewer

A mix of activities. Is there anything about here that isn't so good?

Jack

Just being here really. Like, cos, I don't really want to be here but it's something that's happened. It's happened.

Interviewer

Why are you here?

Jack

I was just naughty most of the time for teachers. I don't really know really.

Interviewer

Would you say you were naughty here?

Jack

Not really no.

Interviewer

What was the school you were at called?

Jack

Greenfield.

Interviewer

Would you say you were naughty there?

Jack

Yeah, most of the time. I didn't like it there. That's why.

Interviewer

You were naughty cos you didn't like it there? What didn't you like about Greenfield?

Jack

I didn't like none of the teachers. I just didn't like it.

Interviewer

Any particular reason about the teachers you didn't like?

Jack

No. Just I was, no. Just the teachers.

Interviewer

So, did you find you didn't get on well with the teachers?

Jack

Not really. I didn't like them, no.

Interviewer

It sounds like you like some of the teachers here?

Jack

Yeah.

Interviewer

Okay. What about the work at Greenfield? Was that different to here?

Jack

Yeah. It was easier there but I didn't used to learn nothing really. It was too easy most of the time.

Interviewer

You found the work at Greenfield too easy.

Jack

Yeah.

Interviewer

And you find the work here harder?

Jack

Yeah.

Interviewer

How long have you been here?

Jack

Since year 4, 5.

Interviewer

So that's two years?

Jack

One.

Interviewer

Okay. So what eventually led to you leaving Greenfield? Was there a particular thing happened or...?

Jack

Just cos, being cheeky that day and I didn't want to go to school. And I went to school knowing that I was going to get into trouble anyway. So, I just ...

Interviewer

Did you find it affected how you were at home with mum?

Jack

A bit. Not really though.

Interviewer

So you were being cheeky and you ended up coming here. And you were saying you don't really want to be here?

Jack

No. Yeah, really 'cos it's a PRU.

Interviewer

What does it mean, being in a PRU to you?

Jack

Mostly really naughty kids go there. That's it.

Interviewer

So you don't feel..... What do you think about going to Grove?

Jack

It's better 'cos I like doing sports and everything.

Interviewer

Are you nervous at all?

Jack

Not really 'cos I've been there. I've been loads of times 'cos of my brothers and sisters.

Interviewer

How might you get on with the teachers there?

Jack

Good. 'Cos most of them I already know. I know their names and I go there when my brother used to have parents' evening. I used to go. So that's it.

Interviewer

Are you looking forward to it?

Jack

Yeah.

Interviewer

What are your plans for the summer holidays?

Jack

Probably go on holiday.

Interviewer

Have you got friends here?

Jack

Yeah.

Interviewer

Is it easy to get on with friends here?

Jack

Yeah. There's not many people here anyway.

Interviewer

Quite small classes. Not so many. What were the pupils at Greenfield like?

Jack

I didn't like most of them.

Interviewer

Why?

Jack

Just like they used to say stuff and then laugh and that. Just being stupid.

Interviewer

Teasing you?

Jack

I can't really remember. Just that they did used to do it. All the time.

Interviewer

Did you ever tell the teachers?

Jack

Not really no.

Interviewer

Is there anything else you can tell me about here?

Jack

Not really. You learn a lot.

Interviewer

Are the lessons similar to Greenfield?

Jack

Yeah but it's better for me here. Better, just because I stay in one place for not long.

Interviewer

They change the activities a lot so you do different things?

Jack

Yeah.

Interviewer

Is there anything else you'd like to say?

Jack

Not really, just people who are being naughty and that just should stop because you don't want to end up here. But I already have and I can't do nothing about it. Really it's not long for me to be here anyway. I'm not really bothered.

Interview 4 – Head teacher of excluding school

Interviewer

If you could just tell me a little bit about Jack. When he first started here, if you can remember, and the process of what happened?

Head teacher

Okay. Jack came with a history. He came from Greenfield which is the school next door and when that year group first started he didn't come. There was some mix up with forms and things and he hadn't got a place here at the time. And there was a certain amount of relief in the year group that he wasn't coming. But then that was sorted out and he got a place here but didn't start until it was almost Christmas. During that period he didn't go to school at all, from my memory, and when he did come he had an impact. He's obviously got into a certain pattern of behaviour in the Infant school. He genuinely was quite a nice lad, sunny disposition but he did rule the roost. He did have the sort of mentality that he wanted to be in charge of what was going on. The other children were quite often quite afraid of him. He could be aggressive. He did say a lot of things. He generally had the disposition of a child who was much older. He's the youngest of a family where there is quite a gap

113

between him and the next one. There's a big gap between him and his older brother who he often spent a lot of time with outside as well. And he settled in okay, but as I said he was generally on the playground quite disruptive, quite rough and played games where he ended up hurting people if he couldn't get his own way; lost his temper and hurt other children. And he was okay really for the first year, year 3.

He had a good teacher who managed him very well but as time went on he became more and more aggressive and more unwilling to do, to sit in lessons, to do work and would often attack the other children for no real reason. If he was sent, for example to go and sharpen his pencil or something like that, he would go the long way around so he could bop a few children on the head as he went past. That was his sort of behaviour. He was constantly looking for attention in that way, so he was sort of almost controlling of the other children in the year group. And as the years went on until the end of year 5, when he didn't make the end of year 5 with us; he'd gone to the PRU by then.

I was dealing with complaints from other parents on probably at the rate of two to three a week, to do with Jack's attacking of other children and it was quite violent. It was the sort of thing where he'd push them up against the wall and hold them by the throat type of stuff. It was lots of things he would say. Language which would be at the time I would have associated with much older children, the language he used. He'd often walk out of lessons and go and hide somewhere. Or go for a walk around school and not go back into class. That sort of thing.

And as he moved through the school he became more aware, as often these children do, that because of his behaviour he was behind in his academic work. The realisation of that and the gap between himself and what his peers could do, made it more difficult for him to engage because he didn't want to fail. And that meant that he didn't even try. He would start playing up straight away as soon as he couldn't do something or it wasn't something he wanted to do. If it was art and he was quite happy, he'd get on with it. If it was some numeracy work he couldn't access, because he'd got a very well developed perception of himself as a young sort of teenager, I think he thought of himself. It was very much difficult for him to be seen not to be getting it right and there was a lot of bravado and a lot of that sort of behaviour you get from older lads. He was very mature in that respect. Very self-conscious in fashion terms, often not in uniform, often, and mum was very supportive and tried to get him to wear it. He'd come to school in it but then he'd end up with it not on and something else. And all that sort of stuff and he'd come with a hoodie on some days and he'd be all day with the hood down, that sort of stuff. And he'd walk with an attitude, that sort of street type attitude that older children would have. And we said at the time a lot of it is because he's hanging around with older children outside school. And that was supposition I suppose on our part, but it was that sort of image that we got of him plus a lot of the language and a lot of the behaviour was of children that we often got at the end of year 6, the odd ones that were often out with older children.

But there was also stories about how often he was out hanging around late at night and all that sort of stuff. And whether they're true or not, I've no idea but there was that perception and plus there's a whole lot of background stuff that we knew about and we were informed about. The conflict between mum and dad and the fact that all the sisters were either at home or not at home. All that sort of stuff. But we'd had all the older brothers and sisters come through the school and they were okay. They weren't without their problems but they were nothing like Jack.

Interviewer
What kind of strategies did you try to put in place for him?

Head teacher
There was a great deal of things going on. There was, from a class teachers' point of view, all sorts of behaviour charts. He had a classroom support practitioner assigned to him. There were all sorts of rewards set up, negotiated targets with him. Things that were there for example (shows me a reward chart) for example in 2006, October 2006, which was the year that he ... it sort of started. But there would be times that he did well all morning but he was very much ... I mean I recognise that lady's handwriting ... she would've spent a lot of time out of the class with him, working one to one. A lot of the time he'd be in class to begin with but as soon as he started playing up or not wanting to do it, or disrupting or going around hitting other children. He'd often target individuals. Particular children. And one child in the year group that's just left, he would've been in last year's year 6, was a great big lad. Proper, you know, tough. He had no qualms about going up against him. In fact, you know, part of what he was thinking was 'if I can deal with him, then the rest of them are just going to slip into line'. So he had that no fear of the size of people or whether...

As time went on his language to staff and his language to midday supervisors got worse and worse and worse and he didn't care what he said to anybody, even myself as head teacher. And I was the deputy beforehand. And as a deputy I had much more to do with him from a developmental point of view. That was part of my pastoral role if you like. But when I became head, obviously that wasn't my position and I ended up doing more of the 'he's been sent to me'.

And mum was very supportive and she'd come. But, she'd say we've done this, we've done that, he's been great at home. And then the next time we'd called her in, there'd been an incident and she'd say 'he's been like this for the last two weeks at home'. So his behaviour at home would be up and down. He'd be good, but it was always based on whether Jack was getting what he wanted. So if he'd been bought new trainers and he'd been taken out and they'd done this, that and the other with him, he was okay. And at the time, we didn't have YISP (Youth Inclusion Support Programme, run by the Youth Offending Team), we didn't have that as a facility that we can use here and he would've been a prime candidate for it because we've used it since with two other children that's actually helped them turn their behaviour around.

But that was three years ago now, it wasn't something that was available. It wasn't made known to us. He was, slips into that sort of character, where he was getting into trouble outside school, or he was difficult to handle. He didn't see the need to do any learning. He didn't see that it was actually going to help him get anywhere. He was switched off the whole thing. It was only if it was something he was interested in that he'd actually engage for a while and when we came to the point where we were discussing a move to the PRU, we'd excluded him on a fixed term exclusion twice before for aggressive behaviour towards other children.

Interviewer
Short term?

Head teacher
Yes, we'd done one. A two week I think it was. And we'd got to the stage where we were discussing with the PRU about what could be done next. It was more a matter of... the way we looked at it was what can we do to get him re-engaged before he goes on to high school? Because what will happen when he goes to high school is he'll just be out and won't be in school at all. That was where we were coming from in terms of our work with him and his mum. And that's where mum was very supportive and said that she wants him to be able to get on and learn, but at the moment he's not. He's getting to the point where his behaviour is getting so bad that we would end up following our discipline policy, excluding him permanently. And so it was a managed move to the PRU.

And I believe now he's gone back into high school so in that respect it's worked. It's actually done ... It was an intervention strategy, if you like, to get him back on track so that he can access high school. Had he gone on, I think what would have happened here, is we would've ended up just containing him with support, either in class or out of class. There were days when he wasn't here, days when he was sent home but that would've gone on to the end of year 6. He'd have gone to high school and probably not lasted very long at all. That's what we were thinking of in the long term about how we can get him to re-engage rather than how we can get rid of him from here. Bearing in mind we'd got a long history with the family.

All of the other children had gone through so we'd got a good relationship with the family, good relationship with mum and the older brothers and sisters would have to come and get him when he was being sent home when mum wasn't available. So they knew what the score was. And a lot of what we'd heard about what he'd seen or he'd witnessed at home or that, we could understand why he was the way he was. But in the context of 250 children and him attacking them and us dealing with complaints from those children and their parents ...They were saying 'what has to be done before this child's excluded?' You know, you can't just kick them out. You've got to put all these things in place and we did have a great deal of strategies in place for him. There were behavioural charts and programmes and negotiated targets with him. Things that he had to earn and as you can see here (shows example of reward chart) he'd have to earn his football at the end of the day.

So there was ten minutes of football if he'd got enough stickers over the preceding lessons. Where he had a bad time it was, you know, walked out of a lesson (shows another chart), science assessment, he'd never do any tests. He's kept out of a lesson because of the first lesson, you know he played up. 'Started off really well, managed to do lots of writing but towards the end became really silly and graffitied over his book.' So there almost times when he couldn't maintain what he'd started off well and then he's lost it. He didn't want to do the work. That was one of his big problems.

Interviewer

Do you think perhaps he'd have greater ability if he'd focused on it or had he gone to such a point he couldn't have caught up anyway?

Head teacher

No. I don't think he was as bad as he thought he was. I think he got in a mindset where he thought 'I can't do this. What's the point?' and 'I'm not having that lot laugh at me because I can't do it.' And as with lots of special needs children, it became a special needs issue which began with his behaviour but became academic because he'd missed out so much of the work. He got to the point of view that he couldn't do it because there were times when I'd seen his book and he'd been down to me for a gold star. You know, he'd done a good piece of work but he couldn't maintain that.

And the other thing we noticed about him, he wasn't very good at receiving praise. It almost embarrassed him. He couldn't. And even when we'd realised this and given it in the sort of way that we thought he'd be able to cope with. He certainly couldn't cope with anybody saying 'look at Jack's work. Isn't it fantastic? He worked really hard this morning.'

And even the peer pressure things where he was earning things that the rest of the class would benefit from, he couldn't cope with that. Whereas, other children, that's one of the things that gets them going. They get their mates on their side because they've earned extra play for everyone. He couldn't cope with that. He couldn't cope with earning things, like if there was a disco coming up and whether he'd be allowed to go to it or not. He would have to earn it and I'd say, 'right you've got three chances and you'll get there'. He couldn't. Even when he was on track to do it there'd be a point where he'd just blow it. He never could deal with the pressure or the feeling that I'm actually going to succeed here. It's be gone before ... and even when he was ...

Some of the things he blew straight away because he just wasn't interested in even trying but other things he'd try for and then he was getting so close, it was almost as if he didn't believe he was going to get it anyway, I think. And he couldn't cope with that. He couldn't cope with ... even when you were assigning a sort of mentor, from the point of view of another child, he couldn't. It's almost as if he stopped himself trying to be like them. He tried the opposite, that didn't work. We got a learning mentor here who worked with him as well, and she got on quite well with him, getting around him, but he'd spend an awful lot of time out of class then having chats and discussions about why he's behaved like that and try to bring him around and tried to bring him back into class and then he'd do the whole thing again so he'd be out again because he'd prefer to be out. Wandering around. And as time went on he became more and more difficult.

You know at first he'd ended up always doing what I told him to do, but he came in the end when he wasn't even doing ... in the end, he'd be sent to me as Head – I'd talk to him and I'd say 'right, this is what we're going to do' and all of that, negotiate things and go back into class and he'd be alright then for another while and then the next day there'd be another incident but as time went on, I'd be sent for to take him out of class. He'd refuse to come, all that sort of stuff, so it became increasingly difficult to manage. And then you're in the position where the head teacher's coming into the room and you're asking the child to come with you to the office, or to go to see the mentor or whatever, and they're refusing.

Then it becomes increasingly difficult because you're in the position where the children are thinking, 'well, you're not doing what the head's asking you to do ... what happens next?' It's at that point that you start talking about either exclusion or a managed move or something else because he's not going to do what I'm telling him. Where are we actually going to go from here? And it came to a head really when he'd attacked somebody in the corridor and he was doing this more and more often and was becoming more and more violent, that we ended up talking ... we were talking permanent exclusion because it was the end of a long road of exclusions and then we negotiated this managed move to the PRU where he's been for 18 months, before he's moved back in now.

You know, mum didn't want it at the time. She didn't want him to go. She wanted him to stay here, all the other children having been here. It was a big step and also the admission is a real problem and the PRU has a whole stigma attached to it that creates more difficulty. But that was the picture we had, as it became more and more violent. But we understood. We tried to understand a lot of what the background was and what he'd seen and what he'd been, what he'd experienced. Of what we'd been told he'd experienced, allegedly experienced. And in that context you understand why he'd been angry and a disaffected young boy. You can understand that but you don't know how much of that actually happened or whether it was worse than that. And we only got the information that mum was happy to share with us from that perspective. And I think, had he not gone and done ... and I don't know how he'll get on at high school and certainly the fact that he'd have been picked up early, mid-way through primary school, the fact that he's been to the PRU, the fact that he's gone to school with support will certainly help him.

Had we continued the situation to the end of year 6, when he went off, which has happened here in the past. We've had very difficult children where we've had 25 hours of support for them but it's only been a containment situation. They've gone to high school and I'm seeing them walking past here, playing out, mid-morning and thinking 'well he's not in school' and you find out that he's been excluded from his secondary school. Where there seems to be far less tolerance, less sort of chances if you like, we have more chances in Primary school. It's much more sort of looked at, because it's developmental and 'they'll grow out of it' – there's all that side to things.

But certainly since I've been working in the senior management level, the behaviour of children where it becomes troublesome and disruptive is getting earlier. It is a much younger phenomenon. Usually it was the end of year 6, post SATS where a few of them would go and think 'well, I don't have to do any work now. I don't have to do as I'm told, I'm too big for the place. I'm going to high school' and you deal with them for the last six weeks and some of them would end up not finishing the year with you. Now, we had it from year 3 and we had other children as well that have had those sort of difficulties starting very early and we were warned before they get to us that he was going to be... you know. And over the last few years we've had increasingly, a vast increase in the numbers of ADHD diagnosed children in school. In fact, when I became head there were four classroom assistants in school, in the junior school.

There's now eight class teachers, a deputy and myself. There's now nine classroom support people dealing with children with emotional and behavioural problems. And that's grown, partly grown as there's an increase in diagnosis I think, but it's because there's an increase in the number of children that exhibit challenging behaviour and at a much younger age. I mean at the time he was quite, he stood out quite a lot because he was young and exhibiting behaviour that we had experienced with older children. So that created the problems and part of what we thought was that by the time he gets to year 6 he's going to be totally unhandleable and we'll be unable to handle him in any way because he couldn't care less at that stage.

Interviewer

It sounds very much as if the managed move was to get him on track before he completely fell off the track?

Head teacher

Yeah. And I think Mum was having more difficulty with controlling him. A lot of it was down to the older brother I think, in terms of talking with him and dealing with him because he was getting more aggressive and getting bigger with it and it became more of a problem. But, the managed move, we were talking permanent exclusion but then at the time we thought, what actually happens if we exclude him? There's going to be further issues about what happens to him then. Which school does he go to? Is he going to carry on with the same behaviour? So the managed move in that context, eighteen months on, has worked. It worked for the year group as well which was the other side of the coin for us. What is the impact of this child's behaviour on the rest of the children and when you're dealing with somebody who is disrupting lessons all the time, we've got the problem that these children aren't always safe but also they're not making any progress because every time there is a lesson going on that he's decided to kick off in, nobody learns anything. The teacher's whole attention is diverted to him and the class in that year group actually became very self sufficient in terms of, because their behaviour was modified to 'here we go again, we just have to get on'.

So they learned how to get on and they left last year and they were a lovely group over all. They were very independent and self sufficient in that respect but a part of it, not exclusively, but a part of it is because a lot of attention was directed towards Jack and the other children like him in the year group who needed the teachers' attention during lessons. If you've either got to sit next to this child to get him to do some work or right next to him to stop him attacking the other children, then you can't teach the rest of the group. And again, you've got to look at it in the context of how, if we don't do something now for Jack, to move him to a better place to make progress, he's not going to make the progress he's supposed to make and also it's going to have a negative impact on all those other learners. So that's part of the decisions we have to make.

Interviewer
It's not in isolation is it?

Head teacher
It never can be in terms of children having an impact. You've got to do what's best for them but also what's best for the majority. And the pressure of results. And that is an added thing, that you can't turn around at the end of the day and say a child like Jack was in the class and it's had a big impact. You have to act to do something. It was also ... we here pride ourselves on being inclusive and having all of these strategies to help support children but it comes to the point where you have to say of each one, who are we being inclusive for? Just him at the expense of everybody else or is it inclusive for those other children too? And we felt that it was getting to the point that it wasn't.

Interviewer
Were there any other support mechanisms or things that might have helped Jack? You've mentioned YISP (Youth Inclusion Support Programme).

Head teacher
I think at the time it was quite new, certainly in the school to have someone so young behaving like they did. And Behaviour Support had their inputs but it was almost as if they didn't quite know what to do with somebody that young because they're used to dealing with Year 6 and those in the second half of the year. And I think some of the strategies we were asked to do were sort of nothing more different than what teachers were doing anyway. Behaviour charts, well that only works for so long. What do you do next when that one's out? When the novelty of ten minutes football has...

Well, it's alright saying you get ten minutes football at the end of the day if you've earned all your stickers and you've got your targets, but if it's pouring down with rain and the child doesn't get football then it doesn't matter to the child. They've not got what you've promised and at the time you think we'll try and do something else but there's PE going on in the hall at that time and there's very little else you can do. Apart from 'do you want to play on the computer?' which is like 'oh no, I wanted football because that is what you promised'. And those sort of systems, they're not legislating for that. That's going to happen because that's life, but children like that don't understand it and I suspect there's been an awful lot of broken promises along the way and we're not helping. We're adding to that by not saying ... so we do try, because we've learnt a lot from children like him. We do try to give choices, you know, if we can't do the football we'll do this instead, so it's in the child's mind early on.

We've learnt a lot over the years about how to handle these types of children and now we've got more of them in school but not as violent as he turned out to be. We had another child here who was very violent also and he went to the PRU in the year before but he was the first child we had with ADHD. Jack didn't have a diagnosis of anything until late on when it was thought that mum had better take him to the doctors and see what really is up with him. There was such a ... so many different things going on for the poor lad in his life. It was hard to pin down what is the problem here? Because there was an awful lot of home background stuff. It won't have helped him to have known that he was unpopular when he started and the relief of the class and the parents when he didn't start with us in year 3. And then the reverse of that when he did come had an impact that we had to manage. It was... we did have a lot of 'well, this went on through the Infants and we didn't think it would happen because he wasn't here and now he's back here it's started again'.

That feeling that you're sending your child to school knowing that they're going to be picked on by another boy was difficult for the parents and difficult then for us to manage in a way that was best for Jack and also best for them. Because parents often are not interested in the perpetrators' welfare. They just want their child to be okay and they want the child to be punished for it. And their idea of punishment was that the child was excluded. I remember having a long discussion with one parent about the fact that you just cannot just exclude him and say that he's not coming back because there's a process, which I explained to them. And they knew then what the process was about but it still wasn't good enough for them because it didn't solve the problem. They wanted him to be gone, for their child to be left alone and they weren't interested at all in Jack. It's human nature, it's quite understandable but we're caught in the middle of that. What used to happen to Jack is he'd be out for a week on an exclusion, he'd come back and he'd be starting again so all of the good work we'd put in ... all of the ... he'd resent having been excluded.

If children like Jack don't get some support and some intervention to get them back into thinking that there is something worth doing in school and there is something they can get out of it in the end, and yes, they're going to have to control their temper and their behaviour along the way but they'll learn how to do it. But to expect them to do 9 to 3.30 sitting on their bottoms in lessons is too much for them and you've got conflicting views because there'll be people saying he should be able to sit there and do it because that's what school is like. You go to school, you sit and learn and you listen to the teacher and you go home again. But for some kids it's not ever going to be ... It's a fact, I think there's more and more of those children. There's always been children who could never sit still and do their work and those were often the ones who either weren't in school or left very early and did other things. Raising the age to 18, which is what he will have to do, to stay in training until he's 18; they're going to have to come up with something that gives him a reason to be there.

Because his aspirations when he was here is that he's going to have a big BMW and he's going to have this, that and the other and you could see it. He was forever coming to school and I was taking something off him, jewellery that he shouldn't have on. Wherever that came from, whether it was the media or members of the family. That's where he was going. So he couldn't see what, past school, what was going to help him get there.

He was just very very difficult from a classroom management point of view but to be fair to mum you used to ring her up and she'd come and get him, she'd tell him off, she'd take him home. She'd bring him back the next day for a fresh start and we did that quite a lot, but it came to the point where he was out more than he was in. Half ten every day you'd be going 'can you come and get him?' because it got to almost playtime or he'd get to the end of first play, he'd done this, that and the other. And you couldn't tell him off, he couldn't deal with the issues. If he'd had a fight at playtime and hurt somebody and he'd been sent to my room and I'd say, 'what've you done?' He wouldn't be able to tell me. He'd be too angry, huffing and puffing and it would take until twenty past eleven for him to say what's gone on and nine times out of ten he was the perpetrator. He was the one who started it and finished it. He wasn't the sort 'he hit me first so I hit him back .' That's another hour I've wasted trying to deal with one child who can't get it right and then it's almost lunchtime, so he's go out of the whole of that lesson now while I've dealt with it. So he goes back for twenty minutes, causes more problems. It was that all the time and then lunch time – what can I do for an hour with him then? I used to have him in here with me most of the time. There was a period then when I had him going home for dinners because his behaviour at lunchtime, we couldn't ... he'd be troublesome in the dining-room, hitting people, throwing food, that sort of thing. So you'd have to say, 'you can't go out on the playground then.' We're lucky as there's a quiet area here but then you can't have anyone else there, so he'd play up in there or he'd escape to the playground then I'm off searching for him and sending him in and he won't come in. You know, you spend an awful lot of time dealing with that and he learnt very very quickly the patterns of what went on and what happens next. And he knows that if I get into trouble now I'll be outside his office until at least half an hour and if I don't answer any of his questions for at least twenty minutes then I know I'll miss next lesson which happens to be numeracy. And he was very clever that way in terms of being able to manipulate the situation.

Interviewer

Like you say, manipulating and being chased around? Is there anything else?

Head teacher

We used to say about Jack that he'd eventually go a long way. Because he's a good looking lad, he had a lovely smile and he used to be able to use that to his benefit as well. And he would be, when he was in the right frame of mind, you could talk to him. He was that sort of mixture that you thought you can actually get through to him. There's a nice side to him. He has that, enough self-belief in himself to talk to people, but you always felt it was learned behaviour. He'd learnt. He was the youngest in the family by quite a long way. He'd obviously learned early on. His cuteness, if you like, was to his benefit. and he did have that nice side to him but he just couldn't maintain it. It wasn't the thing at the forefront of his persona, it was something that he was almost reluctant to let develop. In a way I suspect it was something he actually thought that it was more him to be one of the bad ones, always in trouble. He adores his mum and I think he'd prefer to be with mum than here. It didn't bother him for me to send for mum. She did dote on him. She told him off when he was sent home and all that sort of stuff but I never knew how far it went when he went home. I don't think sanctions were put in place that would have an impact over a longer period. I think there was a short, sharp shock. But it wasn't very long before it was all back to normal. That's what I suspect.

And mum can't be blamed for that in any way, I think. It's just the way the family operates. Most families tell their ... You tell your child off for doing something wrong but you don't keep it going for two weeks. It's something that's over and done with because you want to get back to normal don't you? And I think that's more or less what happened there. I think other people thought that now he's been excluded, he'll be grounded, there'll be this taken off him, that taken off him. In some households it would have gone further than it did with Jack. I think he was told off and there was a certain amount of time he was in the dog house, if you like, but I don't think it lasted too long because of the mother-son relationship. It's the same in most families. They'll do the telling off for a bit but then let's get it back to normal because we don't want the conflict and that's totally normal, I think. You just used to get the impression that it didn't really bother him.

That whole role model thing we haven't even touched on. His older brother wasn't an angel here, but he was a nice enough lad. He was nothing like Jack in terms of behaviour and we suspected that he became Jack's role model as he was the older one and the dad wasn't there for most of that time. And he didn't have the role models that other children have, but having said that, in this school there's a lot of one parent families where children are with mum or Nan even and so the role model thing I don't know where he got them. He must have got them from somewhere because what we saw, jewellery, the clothes. He was interested in typical male stuff, but you don't know if it was older kids he was out with or his older brother, or media stuff he was into. We think he'd benefit if he went to high school and there was a male mentor or something like that. He's the type that would benefit from that. But, it's a strategy in terms of other children that you need to be able to call on, or something similar more easily than we are at the moment.

As I said earlier on, we waited nearly a whole academic year for one child to get a place in the PRU, where there are eighteen places, to start now and he's only really a priority now because he's reached year 6. Whereas, other children, the intervention because it's all shunting down earlier on, the intervention needs to come in earlier and even if we're talking part time places in PRUs and that sort of intervention where they're going and much more closer working with the PRU in terms of their practices and the practices in the school, so we have that duality in terms of the approach that backs up; but we don't have either the manpower or the general outlook and in a mainstream school the bits that we've tried where we've had different curriculums and different timetables and that, it's actually been to the detriment of other children as they've seen that as being an advantage. They're actually getting more fun. They're doing more football, they're doing more playing on computer games than we are and we're behaving.

So there is that balance we have to strike between developing what is needed for that particular child with all the rewards and things to get them on track and motivate them but in the context of all those other children who are sitting in their lessons and getting on with it and might as well be as bored at times as the children like Jack might be ... Four have had, when I was deputy, I had a group one year of five boys that I had over lunchtime that was the opposite way around for them. They would play first and eat last because they couldn't cope on the playground.

With some parents you never get there, they just don't want to. They're in denial that there is a problem with this child. 'He's not like this at home, he's great at home.' Except he's not here. And when they say they're entitled to full-time education, yes, they are, but not necessarily here and that's what you have to say and you get to the point where you say, 'you're absolutely right but not here'.

Interviewer

It's got to be full-time education in the right place for the child.

Head teacher

The needs of the child have to come first so you have to deal with that. But those are generally from parents who have a negative outlook on school life, so perhaps that's their experiences as well. They're difficult to engage. But lots of these children we have trouble with there is that hole that the child has been lost in conflict between the parents and I think that if there was a study done, I don't know if there has been, based on the correlation between troublesome children and those from split or broken homes, you'll see that there is a definite link. There are a number of children who've gone through splits in this school and they've done fine. It's not always just the fact that they've split. It's the fact that how it happened, and how the child is placed with all that's going on. It's not a generalisation to say that if there's a split family there's bound to be a problem with the child. That's not necessarily true but the one's that ... the two children in my history here from being deputy and head, that have been excluded permanently, have all been from split families. I think there's that, it's not the fact that dad is not there, there is that element that the role model's not there and they've been boys as well. But also you can have the role model there but the wrong role model and that doesn't help either.

It is a much broader thing than just the behaviour of one individual child. It's a whole myriad of factors which make that child behave that way and it's all sorts of things based on family background, what's going on at home, what they're seeing that's domestic violence when there's a split family. Where that child is in the family number. Often it's the youngest, where they aren't, the input isn't quite the same level as it was with older children. You think that there are all of these things as well that are going on that make children like that. But with Jack, at the moment it seems to have worked. But I think generally as a policy there needs to be more intervention earlier on of this nature. We've got children coming in Year 3 where I know the infant school have been trying to get help and support for ... and it isn't until we started shouting that something actually happens because they're getting to the point where they're older and a lot of it is, they say it's developmental or they'll grow out of it. But some children, they won't and you can actually see which ones as soon as they get here. Something should have been done earlier on because this isn't a developmental problem, this is something else. And you can see it and the teachers and the staff next door can see it.

And I know a lot of it is linked to money and is down to support and how to support these children but for the people who see things in black and white, they can see that all their special schools are shut and this is where some of those children should be going, which is a very narrow view of things. But on the other hand, there has to be respite from the children and staff in the school and also somewhere different for this child to engage because they've reached the point where they can stay here to the end but it's not going to work any more and I think we're getting to the point where we need to send children to the PRU and there's no places

Like last year one child was supposed to go in November but as soon as it came to the time there was three children from year 6 from other schools who'd taken priority and they'd gone in and filled the places so we got to keep the child. With the support that's fine but basically the support is still following the child around school as they're doing a merry wander, not in lessons, causing havoc and each day we need to make a phone-call to mum to come and fetch them. That's just containment and you just carry on doing that day in, day out and then if there's a major incident, then for three or four days when he's not here and it's back to square one. But that's not going to work in comparison to what's working with Jack and what will work with other children. We can get them back on track and I think that's the most beneficial that we get these children to be successful at high school otherwise they tend to be out on the street; pushed from one school to another.

Children that still think, 'I'm going to get level 5.' They've never had a level 5. They're not likely to get one, but they still think they're going to get one. There's that sort of misunderstanding.

Interviewer
It just happens......

Head teacher
They don't seem to understand there's an awful lot of work or an awful lot of luck in getting spotted at the right time. They don't get that. They think they've got the latest pair of boots or the kit or whatever, or they play for a local team. Nobody actually telling them. But then if they see other people, like Jack, that had all the jewellery and clothes. It's how did you get there? What have you done? It's that sort of system.

There needs to be closer working practices between these strategies like the PRUs and what's going on in the school. Sometimes they might need to come to school for their lessons bit and somewhere else for their social side and their emotional development. Schools can't do all of it because they're too closely linked in some respects. But I think the emotional needs outweigh their learning and they need to do that somewhere else. Because the teacher can't do it because they've got 30 children to teach and I think that's part of the problem. That the expectation is on teachers to do all of these things whilst raising standards and getting certain grades is too great, and then the child doesn't get it emotionally, then you've got trouble in the classroom and that creates a great deal of conflict for teachers. And then they end up having to deal with things at break time or lunchtime or see parents after school. It's too late for that child then because basically you need to tell them what's going on and it shouldn't happen again. It's not dealing with his emotional needs.

And more and more schools are taking over that role because it's not being done at home and that's how teachers are being trained on that. It's not part of your basic teacher training, you get more on it. You do an awful lot of social work, both for parents and for the children and then it's not something you're trained in. As I said, it's a massive issue, in terms of how teachers cope with it and how schools cope with it. We're getting better at it, but I do feel a lot of it is reactive and just containment as opposed to spotting the problem earlier on and putting in the right people at the right time to deal with it.

6

David

D avid is a white male. He was permanently excluded from school during year 9 but there was a history of difficulties going back to Primary School. The permanent exclusion was as a result of David having a fight with another pupil outside the school gates.

After his exclusion, David's mother requested a multi agency assessment in order to ascertain whether he was autistic. The outcome of the assessment was that he was not diagnosed with autism, but that it was thought that he did have a severe communication difficulty. David spent some time in two Pupil Referral Units before being re-integrated into another mainstream High School. Statutory assessment was carried out whilst David was placed in the second Pupil Referral Unit and he is now the subject of a statement of special educational needs. At the time of writing up this case example, David was just about to leave school and move on to Further Education College. The author who interviewed David has known David and his mother for two years.

David's account of his exclusion

As noted above, David has a severe communication difficulty. He was asked to draw pictures in order to help elicit some information from him. The interview was carried out with his mother present and he needed a great deal of prompting. He became very distressed when recalling his experiences so the interview was terminated. In the account below P indicates prompt, either from the interviewer or A's mother.

P: So one of the first things that happened when you were excluded from school, was a fight with somebody called Steven? Tell me a bit about it.

D: I can't remember it.

P: Can't you remember what started the fight?

D: No.

P: Can you remember where it was?

D: In the new block.

P: OK, so what happened then with you and Steven?

D: Fight.

P: Can you remember what got you angry?

D: He punched me.

P: So Steven started it off, he punched you first?

D: Hmm.

P: Did he say anything to you to make you angry or did he just punch you?

D: I don't know.

P: Was anything done after you had that fight with Steven?

D: I don't know.

P: Can we have a look at this picture now? This one, this is the thing that happened just outside the school gates. Tell me about that. I can see you have drawn a house and car so was that right outside the school gates?

P: How did you see Steven that day?

D: All right he was fine.

D: To start with there was then they went and I saw him.

P: OK so you saw him. What made you go down to him?

D: I don't know.

P: So you walked down the road and saw Steven, and then what?

D: He was fine again.

P: Did you start it this time?

D: Hmm.

P: Why were you still angry with him?

D: I dunno.

P: Do you feel uncomfortable answering these questions? You're not in trouble.

Interview terminated at this point because David was becoming very distressed.

David's mother's account of his exclusion

David's mother was first of all asked to say a little about his early years and development, because she felt very strongly that David had experienced difficulties from a very early age but that these difficulties had not been recognised or taken seriously.

I have got four lads and they are all different in other ways, but David was completely off the scale and the other thing was he was very hyperactive but I noticed there was also repetition in what he did. From a young age he loved art and from the age of two he would sit on top of the landing, and he would always sit on top of the landing in the same spot, and draw volcanoes. Now from my experience as a mom my children all started off with houses and circles and scribble and trees and mommy and daddy, not David, was a volcano with lots of curly lava and they were all the same and they were all about the same size on the paper and he would come and show it me not wait and ask whether that's lovely it was 'here are' and gone, gone to do the next one.

Up until Year 5 when I started experiencing problems with him David was a very quiet, introverted little boy and was not the sort to put his hand up and answer any questions in class. When I first asked teachers how he was doing they told me he was making little progress but in little steps. When he got to Year 5 David started running away from school and to initiate any kind of confrontation whether it be pupils or staff he would jump over the wall and either come home or run up to the park if I wasn't home. I had a series of phone calls from the Head saying that David wouldn't comply to their rules but David was hitting out at other pupils. Several times David had two-day exclusions in which I would go down and pick him up. I wasn't aware until I went to help David out, I actually went into Year 5 to sit with him every day from 9.00 to 3.00 just to see how David was coping because he certainly wasn't the same lad at school as he was at home. In fact I was quite horrified to find that he wasn't coping at all, he couldn't sit in a chair for long periods, he was constantly told off by the staff, he was sent outside the classroom on a few days.

I realised then there was something very, very wrong even though I knew David had severe communication difficulties which was expressed to the school it wasn't picked up on. I know at one point the advisory teacher for learning and the advisory teacher for behaviour went in and one has told me that David just wanted more attention from his mom which I disagreed with. As soon as I started sitting with David his confidence was a lot better it was almost like a sigh of relief when I came in and sat with him. In work he managed to jump up two levels in one year but he was still not getting along with other children and I found that a lot of the children knew which buttons to press with David and then it would all go bosh and then again he would be excluded for a couple of days.

Again I told them I've got issues about his communication difficulties in which they disagreed and I said have you noticed him just doing 'yes', 'no' and 'I don't know' but it's not explaining anything and again they said no they hadn't noticed anything like that, I said but he's not explaining anything if you ask him.

I also noticed that when a teacher asked him a question he would go hand to mouth and there was many times that he ran out of the classroom and I asked the teacher was it often that David did this and she says 'oh yes, he doesn't like being asked question, but he has got to accept that he will be asked questions which again I said well doesn't that seem kind of strange? I think that what the school put it down to was the fact that they were aware that I did have difficulties at home with David's dad and I think they looked at it as a home problem and I think they put it down to things that David had witnessed as a young child, had made him like this and had made him stubborn and aggressive towards other people.

When I went in school with him I did question that, I know they weren't happy with me questioning that but I said this is not all down to my parenting and although I hadn't made the right choice in David's dad and what was happening at home I knew as a mother that it wasn't down to my parenting, I knew I wasn't the best mom in the world but I knew I was a good mom.

When he got to Year 6 I said to the Headmaster I need to be in a different room from David because he's going to High School he's got to be away from me because I can't sit in with him in lessons at High School, so they took me on as an assistant for another child at the Primary when David got into Year 6, and the Head said I am sorry you are just going to have to go with him because he just won't tolerate you not being in there with him and I said well he's not going to learn anything by that, as long as he knows I am still in the school that should be enough if things get tough but being the person I was I went in and I sat in with David still which in hindsight now that was so wrong.

David still got into fights, he didn't like being laughed at, he got embarrassed very, very easily, that was one emotion he could show and he could show well, that and anger. I can understand where the anger came from because he couldn't verbally shout out really, but again in the class was a very rude, insolent boy which I completely disagreed with. By this time dad had left as well, David didn't cope very well with dad leaving and would often be violent towards me like it was my fault that dad had left.

David's mother then went on to describe what happened after David transferred to High School.

When he went to high school I got in touch with his Head of Year and explained the situation. I really couldn't have expressed it any more to the Head of Year about David's communication difficulties and how that has an impact on his behaviour. It's a shame that the Head of Year sees everything in black and white although he was very good he was less tolerant. So of course David did cop the brunt of that. Also because of the way other people perceive David they also got different kind of information up in secondary, so primary told secondary that David's just a spoilt boy, he doesn't know the word 'no'. So in the first year I was amazed how he did cope for the first year. I moved up with David but also with this other lad I was supporting so then it didn't look as bad on David but what I refused to do point blank was sit in a room with David.

When things went wrong I would always express to David you have got to follow rules, you can't just do what you want to do. David ended up being drawn to the wrong kind of people and it's really wrong of me to say that because some of these kids also had the same kind of difficulties, they couldn't sit for long in a chair. David just started playing about with all these risk takers that were pretty good with communication where David wasn't and they loved David because they would only have to ask David something and he would do it, and David was loyal to them because finally he got some friends.

The first six months he managed, I don't know how he got through it but he did manage with support, they did support him but he was kept in low ability classes and that's where again I think things go bosh because there isn't enough support and I can understand that, we had to share the support with all the rest of the pupils who struggle so a lot of kids that are capable of being quite functional don't end up in the higher sets because they have to be kept down where the support is. And David needed to get up out of his seat even if it was to get a sharpener just something to move about. This didn't go down very well because the rules of sitting down and have your own sharpener and have your own rubber, you are not allowed to get out of your seat. In the end his Head of Year did make him a card so that if things got too rough he could go outside but David liked it outside in the corridor it was better, he could move about, he could walk up and down the corridor if he wanted to and he wasn't restricted to a desk, a chair and the real struggle of having to do English and lots of writing which he couldn't cope with.

It wasn't until he got to Year 9 in which he was in a series of fights because he was hanging about with quite a big group they wanted to split this group up and the first name that came up was David let's get rid of David because they used David the rest of them used David and David does what they say he's loyal to them.

The PRU manager's account

I never picked David up from the moment he was excluded, he went to another PRU and there was an incident there of a violent nature. We were not a PRU at that moment in time we were the reintegration team and I was asked if the team would work with David. Because of the past record that had been described to me and the incident that had occurred previously I said that I would not have him on a full time basis but would have him on a small one-to-one timetable in order to investigate what he was like at that point in time.

I was expecting a very violent individual by the way he had been described and through his school file which had various weapons in it and obviously incidents that described somebody of a violent nature, so I actually didn't know what I was going to receive and often things that are written down when you actually get the person in front of you they are totally different from what they are described as. When we started to look through his files there was no Primary School information, the file had gone missing and we knew that he had experienced difficulties in his last two years at Primary School. Consequently it was difficult to find evidence to help us identify what his needs were.

So he came into me on a very personalised timetable, he wasn't in a social group with other pupils he was on a one-to-one basis. We set about teaching the basic core subjects, maths, English, identifying what he liked and trying to engage him through that. It soon became apparent that David wasn't the person that was described in the file. He took everything literally and there were certain people he could work with and there were certain people that he couldn't and if you looked at who he could work with and the reasons why he could work with them and who he couldn't work with we soon realised there was a communication difficulty there. The other thing that became very apparent was the fact that he never asked why he wasn't with other pupils.

That brought a question mark up, why did that conversation never take place and he never asked when he was actually going to get to work with other pupils. He was just happy to go along with what was presented in front of him. As we did various things with him we realised that one of David's difficulties was the 'flight and fight' scenario. When he found himself in a very difficult situation that he couldn't actually communicate verbally that he had a problem, he would get into a confrontation where he would want to leave at all cost. We learned to recognise the warning signals and we would back off. He wasn't at that stage yet where he could verbalise his difficulty to us. We built up a really, really good relationship with him and eventually he was able to tell us that he could not communicate his problem.

I'm not saying it was easy, it was quite hard going, working one-to-one and trying to motivate him to do English when he has communication difficulties. We soon realised this was something different, he wasn't your normal behavioural kid there were other issues going on.

I think the difficulties with a large establishment like a High School was that they didn't know him as well as we got to know him so therefore they couldn't actually see the differences they just deemed him to be a behavioural difficulty and really couldn't see the reasons behind it.

He was with us until the end of Year 9. We had requested a formal assessment of his needs but the process was not completed and he left us without having a placement anywhere. Eventually what happened is that Slater Road High School were approached and they agreed to take David on. Fortunately we were doing a service level agreement with Slater Road High School so it enabled us to actually support him so we were with him every step of the way until we could actually stand back and say 'right now it's over to you'. By the time we backed off the statement was complete he had been diagnosed with a communication difficulty and a specialist team became involved to forward plan for when he actually left school.

The PRU manager's reflections on David's exclusion

Well obviously, every exclusion is different and when you read the case files you often wonder how the exclusion was allowed to go through and how it got through the governors?

I have ranted and raved about governor training, there needs to be an understanding of what happens to a pupil when they are excluded and what their chances are out there, particularly when they have been identified as having learning difficulties earlier on, or medical difficulties. Working with David enabled us to look at every kid with a possibility that they could be like him, it skilled us up.

We worked closely with mum, we talked and talked and talked about David and there was a realisation that what had gone on at home in the past had affected what had gone on at school. If mum hadn't have fought for David to have his needs met, I don't think he would have had them met.

The school account: interview with the SENCo

David was a difficult child to work with when he started, he had quite severe literacy difficulties, huge hang ups. His perception of what he could do he was convinced that he couldn't read, he couldn't write and a whole load of behaviour baggage that came along with it. He presented as a very, very angry young man with a barrier up wanting to keep the world at bay and it took us a long, long time to form a relationship with him. It was made complicated in school because his mum worked with us as an LSA as well, and I think she was put in a difficult position sometimes because having her here immediately she knew that David's done this, David's done that, this has kicked off, where normally you'd think before you got in touch with parents, if you've got to pick up the phone you wait a little bit.

He got through Year 7 reasonably well, then went into Year 8 and the problems really started to kick off. He's got a very, very short temper and had a strong friendship with a very dodgy group of lads, had a fierce loyalty to his group of friends, couldn't see that they didn't always do the right thing and weren't always the right influence on him, but wouldn't hear anything bad. I think it was brewing, you could see it coming as he was getting a little bit older, always a little, physically small boy, emotionally a little boy. As he got older he got more of a reputation in school and it just began to snowball. And once kids get a reputation, if you press the right buttons you get a firework show, kids know that and they used to set him off.

The thing that got him into the most trouble though was his resorting to violence to solve a problem, his attitude was that you go in with your fists first and you solve things that way, if you can't solve a problem you fight your way out. And a lot of that was defensive. He got into some quite difficult trouble with male members of staff which I think was linked with the domestic violence issues that he had, he found it very, very difficult to deal with male authority figures particularly if they started to raise their voices. You could see him go into panic mode the moment staff would start to shout.

Account of the specific incident that led to the exclusion

It happened outside of school in the road, with another Year 8 boy. I expect it was six of one and half a dozen of the other, knowing the other lad that was involved, he can be a rogue as well, one had said something about somebody else and they'd gone in and David is quite strong and assaulted the lad and a member of the public witnessed it. And it was then an assault and the police were involved. And unfortunately David has got a record with the police as well, which stacked up against him. There had been low level – cautions that he's had, being in the wrong place at the wrong time, with this gang of lads. The kudos of 'I must be a member of this group' was very, very important to him. I think it was probably the last straw because there'd been a number of quite violent incidents. If it had been another child without that record that particular incident wouldn't have led to a permanent exclusion, but it was the last thing.

Interviewer (I): What happened to the other lad that was involved in the fight? Can you remember?

SENCo: I can't remember to be honest. He's gone on to pretty much get into trouble.

I: So he wasn't permanently excluded?

SENCo: The other boy wasn't, no.

I: But he still continued to be troublesome?

SENCo: Oh yes.

I: So the decision, out of the two, to exclude David was after a series of incidents?

SENCo: Yes.

Reflections on the exclusion

SENCo: When the permanent exclusion did come I felt at the time immense frustration because he was the first pupil we had in the therapy department, he was coming in part time, I was working with him doing some one-to-one counselling work with him. He was beginning to talk to me about family dynamics and how he felt when he was getting angry, beginning to open up when the incident happened, which was partly outside of school and completely out of our control.

Looking back on it perhaps six months later when he was settled it needn't have happened. Far too many people in positions of authority had made their mind up about him – a troubled kid and we've got to get rid of him. I think once people have made their mind up about that there's not a lot you can do.

If David was with us now, he wouldn't have been permanently excluded. He would have gone into the nurture group. He would have had support from that and we could have had a much tighter package around him, to prevent what happened. Which is sad.

7

Sam

Sam was 15 years old at the time of the interviews. He has dual heritage and speaks English as his first language. He was permanently excluded from a high school whilst in Year 8 and has attended a pupil referral unit for Key Stage 3. He was not considered to be able to be returned to a mainstream school and attended the PRU for Key Stage 4. The interviews include his mother, teachers from the school and units involved and learning mentors working at the Key Stage 4 PRU. Sam declined to be interviewed on tape.

Interview 1 – Sam's mother

Interviewer

I'm going to take you back to your pregnancy with Sam and Sam's birth. Talk you through basically Sam's history so far and I want to focus on the exclusion experience. So if I can just take you back to his birth. Was it a normal birth and a normal pregnancy?

Mother

Everything was fine till I was 26 weeks pregnant and then I haemorrhaged. I was obviously taken into hospital and from 26 week until when Sam was born at 37 weeks I was basically bed-ridden. I had, I don't know what the medical word is for it, but it's what they call a low-lying placenta which is high risk to me and the baby. Then I actually went into labour when I was 37 weeks pregnant. Sam was born 26 hours later, it was the most horrendous pain, I mean I had two more children prior to that, the only pain killer I had though was just Pethadine, and he was a big baby, he was 9lbs 7oz born and that was three weeks early so I dread to think what he would have been like if I had gone full term. That was my pregnancy.

Interviewer

And what kind of baby was he?

Mother

He was a good baby. He was pleasant, very rarely got up in the night, very loveable, slept well, ate well. He had eczema, baby eczema which irritated him a lot and it wasn't very nice and then when he got to what they call the 'terrible twos', oh he had such a temper on him, which I know two year olds can have temper tantrums on them but when he had one it was like you literally had to hold him to literally calm him down.

Interviewer

At what age did he walk and talk?

Mother

Quite early actually. I would probably say, well he was walking before he was one I know that, probably saying his first words before that age as well, so he was pretty quick, pretty quick yeah.

Interviewer

By the time he was two he had the terrible twos, he had the tantrums, what happened after that? Did you take him to nursery?

Mother

Yes, he did go to nursery just round the corner from here actually. He went to nursery and obviously his first day at nursery was like, phew, terrible for me, terrible for him. I was crying, he was crying but then he got used to it and he loved it and it went well. He went mornings.

Interviewer

And where did he go to school after that?

Mother

The same school because the nursery is actually on to the school, which was excellent and then obviously he was there through his infants into juniors and it was great. He attended school regular, the teachers were brilliant and no I never had any problems, everything was just normal.

Interviewer

So things were OK in junior school, he transferred to the high school?

Mother

Oh, there is an oh. Oh no, I was thinking of David then, I do apologise, I've got a bit confused in that bit.

Yes he went to the high school, everything seemed fine for a while. He was a bit thingy about going to the high school because I think what it was to be in such a small environment and then to go to a big school and he was concerned that he wouldn't find his classrooms and worrying in general because Sam was the biggest at his school, he was now going to a school where he was going to be not so much the littlest but the youngest and he kind of fretted over that a bit but then he knew a lot of people that went there. His cousins went there, his aunty lived literally round the corner from the school so after a couple of weeks he settled down and seemed to do OK, he did OK.

Interviewer

So at what point where you aware of difficulties arising?

Mother

Well I know exactly when it was. It was August 2006. We had gone on holiday to Brean for a week. There was me and my partner, Sam and my nephew. Up until that point I never had no major issues with Sam, only the general teenage every day, what every parent has, and then I remember we had gone on holiday to Brean, we had a good holiday, we came back and Sam then started to knock about with some people he hadn't been knocking about with prior. He knew them but he had never really had much to do with them and then when we got back off holiday he just started to kind of hang about with different people and I would say it was from that point that things changed and it's embedded in my mind because it happened in August 2006, I know it did, yeah.

Interviewer

So how did it unfold after that?

Mother

Things just got worse. Sam to me was mixing with the wrong people, his attitude changed towards me, towards people, towards school, coming the big I am, swearing, he was just a completely different kid, completely different. I can't recollect him swearing and the bad behaviour and the staying out late prior to that. I am not saying it happened straight away, it kind of built up over a period of time but it did start after we came back off that holiday.

Interviewer

So how did that impact on his life at school?

Mother

Well obviously his behaviour got worse at school, not wanting to go, being disrespectful to me, to teachers, he didn't like the idea of being told 'no' or you have got to this, and it was difficult and it just seemed to get worse and worse it was just a vicious circle. We were all trying to do our best and it was just getting worse and worse and worse.

Interviewer

OK, so just talk me through the exclusion itself.

Mother

Up until the exclusion, or just prior to it, Sam had been getting into trouble quite a lot, I'm not speaking out of turn, Sam knows this anyway, he pinched a mobile phone from the school from a teacher, yes, he did admittedly give it straight back. He said there was no particular reason why he pinched it because I mean he had got a brand new one of his own anyway. Some of his friends, who at that point, had been already expelled from the high school were now going to other schools like S. and different places and some of them wasn't at school I felt like Sam felt that he didn't have to go to school, he was kind of having to live up to what they were doing. This is my own opinion, Sam might think I am wrong, I don't know, and then obviously the school had to think of the other children because being such a big school and Sam was acting in a very, very naughty manner.

Interviewer

What kind of things was he doing?

Mother

Swearing, chucking things, walking out of school, opening exit doors, things like that, threatening, threatening behaviour, never actually took the abuse out on the teacher but would actually threaten them. If he wanted to go home he would just go, end of. If he was grounded it was 'no, I'm going out' and it was just horrendous. Then I got called to the school for this meeting in front of the board of governors and obviously I put my point across because obviously yes there was many things that I didn't agree with what Sam had done and I admitted to the things he had done but also I still didn't want him to get expelled. I was overruled and he had to go and I was absolutely gutted, it was horrible.

Interviewer

What happened after that?

Mother

After that, obviously he was out of school for a while, for a few months.

Interviewer

Months?

Mother

Yes, it was a few months, it was four months, it has got to have been at least four months, if not it could have been a little bit longer but we are talking around a four-month period. They actually then got him into, I think it was [a pupil referral unit].

Interviewer

[PRU name].

Mother

[PRU name], yes. He didn't settle in there very good to be honest, then it was S, which at first didn't seem too bad but then it was the kind of 'I want to do what I want to do, I don't like being told what to do, end of' and it was just a vicious circle again and he got chucked out of there and he just seemed to me to be getting worse and worse and worse, and then he ended up where he is now, the KS4 PRU. I personally, from my own point of view, I mean Sam has been a sod while he's been at the KS3 PRU, he has been a bugger, but I do find out of the high school, KS3 PRU and [a work related project], even though Sam was 'I hate it', I do find they have got a lot more patience at the KS4 PRU, they bend over a lot more, I'm not saying the other schools haven't bent over for Sam, I'm not saying that but they tend to stick with it more, but I think what it is because he has got a mentor as well, Len, I think Len is literally bending over backwards for Sam to keep him in there. I mean there was a period of time when Sam was losing a hell of a lot of time from the KS4 PRU, Sam will tell you being abusive, the chairs chucking, the swearing, the attendance got really, really, really bad you know. They have even put taxis on for him now to get him to and from school, which have been working, so that is a good, positive thing. The taxis have been working so his attendance has got a hell of a lot better. He has been doing well, he's had a bit of a fall back today but nobody can be perfect 100% of the time, but he has been doing good. It's just like ups and downs, ups and downs.

Interviewer

OK, can I just take you back to the group of probably lads he was falling in amongst in that August 2006? Tell me more about them, would you? Tell me more about the group.

Mother

Well, to be honest with you the group of lads he was knocking about with, they went to the high school as well and their names was brought up a lot with the school and in the community with the police. There was all these groups of names and Sam seemed to knocking about with these group of lads and I, yes I know Sam has got his own mind, and Sam hopefully should know right from wrong, but I do think that the people he was knocking about with, he still has a little bit to do with them now but not as much as he was with them at the time, he still sees them now. I don't know whether he was trying to like impress them or be one of them or they were like saying 'Sam, come on, this is the thing to do', I don't know. The group of lads had either been expelled, been suspended, been in trouble with the police, thieving, yeah literally all of them, yeah.

Interviewer

OK, the other area that would be of interest, you mentioned you had got three kids.

Mother

I have got three lads.

Interviewer

Do you live with their father?

Mother

No, me and their father are divorced.

Interviewer

So you are living on your own.

Mother

With my partner.

Interviewer

How old was Sam when his dad left?

Mother

Eleven.

Interviewer

So that's about the same as Primary to Secondary transfer?

Mother

Yes.

Interviewer

Was there any impact of that on Sam?

Mother

At the time everything seemed to be pretty OK but as Sam's got older and as he's been in trouble for different things and Sam has, on a few occasions, been upset and said it's his dad's fault for the way he is and if his dad hadn't have left everything would have been OK. You know when I have tried to explain to Sam, you know, that even though his dad's not here we still love him but we could not just stop together because it just wasn't working. I do feel sorry for him but life has to go on, yeah.

Interviewer

So are all three of your boys still at home?

Mother

No, no, my eldest lad is 23, he's got his own property with his girlfriend, he's a computer technician and his girlfriend is an English teacher. David lives here, he's 18, he's a labourer's scaffolder and then I have got Sam who's at school.

Interviewer

OK. Sam has one more year till he finishes school.

Mother

Yes.

Interviewer

What do you think is going to happen then?

Mother

After school I personally think he will go out and, he wants to work, Sam is a saver, he likes to save money, he likes to buy things. We have got a shed out there which

Sam saved for and bought himself with his pigeons in. Not right down the bottom, here let me show you, Sam actually paid for that himself by saving up. Yeah so I reckon he will go out and work, regardless of what work it is he'll be a grafter and he'll work.

Interviewer

Good. OK let's stop there unless there is something you think you ought to say into the microphone about Sam.

Mother

I think Sam is a little bit misunderstood, I do. He can be a bugger and he can have a really bad temper, you know what I mean? But he's a pussycat inside and he can be a very, very, very loving kid and I love him.

Interviewer

OK, well let's stop on that nice note.

Interview 2 with Manager of LSU – excluding school

Interviewer

Right LSU Manager we are here to talk about Sam and what I'd like you to do is tell me first of all what do you remember around the time Sam was here and what led to the exclusions.

LSU Manager

Sam, when he first came to the high school, was outgoing, quite a bubbly, loud character. I think during Year 7 he was very manageable within the remit of school and responded to the rewards and sanctions that we had in place and I think went through Year 7 without too many major incidents. As he moved through Year 8 he became more disengaged with the whole process of education and classrooms and the rules and the expectations that people had of him within classrooms but on a one-to-one basis he continued to be a very pleasant, cooperative and reasonable young man in many ways and you could remove him from situations, talk to him, calm him down, he was able to verbalise where he had gone wrong, what the issues were and on most occasions you could get him back into classes and then have a period of calm again.

Towards the end of his time with us he was very, very difficult to engage in anything that we at that time had to offer him and because he was still Key Stage 3 we were very limited at that time in what we could offer him. We tried individual work, we tried removing him from mainstream, we tried various different aspects of support but as time went on he became less and less agreeable to engaging with any of it and towards the end we just felt that we hadn't got anything else that we as a school could offer him that would enable him to complete his Key Stage 3 to get the transfer into Key Stage 4 and we just felt we had gone down every avenue that we could with all the people that we had available to us at the time and just felt that we couldn't contain him in a classroom and at that point in time we didn't have enough resources to maintain him out of the classroom.

Interviewer
Was there a critical incident that tipped the balance?

LSU Manager
It was more a build up of incident after incident after incident and the incidents became the constant as opposed to the behaviour, you know everything became a challenge and a confrontation and we couldn't get him to engage.

Interviewer
Were the confrontations with the staff or other kids?

LSU Manager
Both really, more with staff than with kids, but there were and obviously the impact on other kids' education as well was an issue that we had to deal with at the end because wherever he went there was quite a negative impact on everybody else.

Interviewer
You seem to think that Year 7 was containable and manageable. Was there a sudden change in Year 8?

LSU Manager
No, I think it was more gradual, and he was quite a big lad and I think he felt very much that he had to live up to his image, if you like, and he was quite a bit bigger than other kids and sometimes that can cause conflict for the kids themselves because other people view them as being older and more mature and able to handle things and very often, well certainly in Sam's case he was an immature person, but in a man's body and I think that certainly didn't help him in the way other kids and his peer group viewed him because they had expectations of him. I think outside of school as well he was mixing with older people and I know mum was concerned about that at quite a few points along the way.

Interviewer

So what were your theories about Sam?

LSU Manager

Sam, if we could have offered Sam some off-site placement and alternative edu-cation from Year 8, I'm fairly sure we could have saved him, done some worthwhile work with him. I think part of the issue with kids like Sam is that inclusion isn't a cheap option for kids and in order to help kids like Sam you need to have resources that are outside the box of mainstream schools and it takes a lot of input, cash yes, but also people out there who can work with them. I know you have 14 – 19 which is great but for a lot of the kids it's 13ish where you need to be able to start access-ing alternatives to the mainstream in order to be able to maintain them and to try and latch on to the positive and with Sam we had got into a totally negative vibe and it was difficult to find something positive that we could sustain long enough to impact on his behaviour because he had got into a very negative frame of mind and his behaviour became very negative and we really at that point hadn't got anything to sort of counterbalance that out with. I think if we had been able to we could have perhaps maintained his place in the mainstream sector.

Interviewer

OK, let's stop there.

Interview 3 – Manager of Receiving PRU

Interviewer

That's great R (KS4 PRU manager), thank you. Just start by telling us about Sam.

R (KS4 PRU manager)

Sam came here in September last year. He came to our induction day with his mum where he met staff and filled in paperwork and so on. He actually came to us with an exit strategy to go back to mainstream school, I can't remember which one at the moment, he seemed keen to go back to mainstream school and his mum was very keen for him to go back. When he started here that was the basis on which we were working with him that he would be going back to mainstream school. His report from Key Stage 3 Pupil Referral Unit where he hadn't been for very long said that he was a model student and they hadn't had any problems with him whatsoever but he hadn't been there very long. When he started here he was very good, no problems, well behaved for the first couple of weeks. I don't know what happened but that didn't last very long. I think it might have coincided with us talking about him going back to mainstream and saying that we were going to do the paperwork for that, that might have been, I don't know really, but his behaviour changed and he became disruptive and quite aggressive and quite difficult to manage really.

It was suggested when he started here that he had some problems with literacy and numeracy and we were going to give him some one-to-one extra help with that but he resented that and he didn't want the extra help so he made that quite difficult for us as well but his skills weren't as bad as we were led to believe and not nearly as bad as some of the other pupils here so in a way he didn't seem as though he needed that extra help either so he continued to attend here, we couldn't refer him to mainstream because we have to write a report saying that his behaviour has improved and he is ready to go back and it was quite clear that he wasn't ready to go back so he stayed with us. Really his behaviour continued to deteriorate and his attendance has recently really deteriorated.

He lives with his mum, I think he has got an older brother living there as well. His dad, I believe, has got another family, I don't know whether his dad has remarried but he has got another family. Mum and dad are both very, very nice people, very supportive, Sam lives with his mum but sees his dad quite a lot. Having met with both parents and Sam together it is very clear that Sam is extremely fond of his dad and of mum and I suspect that perhaps he found it very difficult them splitting up and that he would like them to be together.

He has got a one-to-one learning mentor at the moment who was appointed about four or five weeks ago who he seems to be relating reasonably well to and he is trying to get Sam to attend the Centre. His mum is at the end of her tether because she obviously doesn't want to get into trouble with the Education Welfare Officer for Sam's non-attendance so things are looking poor on that front really at the moment although there is a meeting this week with his mum and dad and Sam about what we can do to improve his attendance. We may offer him a taxi to get him here because I know it is a dire situation for them all really.

Sam can be a very pleasant young man, he is very big for his age really and I do wonder sometimes if that makes things difficult for him, if he has used that to intimidate people and maybe frighten them or maybe people have related differently to him because he is much bigger. He has been aggressive and has intimidated female members of staff. There was an upset in the ICT room one day when he tipped over a table and threatened Debbie who was teaching the lesson that day. He has been quite aggressive to me on occasions when I have asked him to go to lessons and he has said to me 'move away you, don't stand next to me or I will hurt you' and things like that but he hasn't laid hands on any members of staff but he can be quite intimidating really and shout 'move away, don't come near me, you are in my space', when quite clearly staff aren't in his space. I think he is basically quite an unhappy young man and I think that's all really on who Sam is at the moment.

Interviewer

Let me just ask you about his dad. Have you met him?

R (KS4 PRU manager)

I have met his dad at a meeting, yes.

Interviewer

How would you describe him?

R (KS4 PRU manager)

His dad is a bus driver, a West Indian man, he loves Sam, Sam loves him, I think he is quite laid back. Sam sees him a couple of times a week, if Sam isn't at school or if there are problems mum has requested that we also inform dad so we do do that. I think dad is taking responsibility in that we can ring him and we can request that he comes to meetings and he will do that but it's a little bit on the surface really, the actual responsibility that he is taking for Sam and I believe he has got another family so it's a little bit like lip service really to the problem that we have got and he is saying he is not sure if he can come to the meeting set up this week to discuss Sam. A very, very nice man but I don't think he is taking a lot of responsibility.

Interviewer

What about his mother?

R (KS4 PRU manager)

His mum is a white lady, quite a small lady and Sam is very big. Worries a lot, takes a lot of responsibility, she works at Asda on a fork lift truck, she can't work out what is wrong with Sam, she can't work out what has happened really, why is all this happening, rings here a lot to talk to staff, needs a lot of support. Seems to get on reasonably well with dad but sort of insists that dad should take some responsibility as well, but she takes most of the responsibility and she is stuck really, she doesn't know what to do basically at the moment.

Interviewer

Does Sam have brothers and sisters?

R (KS4 PRU manager)

She did mention that at Christmas there was an older brother that Sam was fighting with, I don't know if there's younger ones. I think there is probably grown up ones and I think his dad has got another family as well.

Interviewer

You mentioned one hypothesis, perhaps two, the first one was that when there was a suggestion that he might go back to mainstream school his behaviour deteriorated and the other was something to do with the marital break-up. Is there anything more around either of those things that springs back to you?

R (KS4 PRU manager)

I think the suggestion ever since he came here really has been his basic skills aren't up to the standard they should be really and that we needed to give him extra help but he made that very difficult for us and he was able to cope well enough in the lessons here. He has put up barriers really, barriers to learning ever since so I don't know whether his skills are very poor and if he found that really difficult at mainstream but he won't let us get near enough to him to find out really so we have had to put that to one side and that might have worried him about going back to mainstream, I think. Yes, I think he is torn between both his parents really and he loves them both and I think that perhaps whatever happened really, I don't know if the parents realised how distressing it was for him, the split-up and you can tell that he was so pleased when his dad came to school and he obviously loves both of them and I think he finds it very difficult.

Interview 4 – Mentors working at PRU

Interviewer

The first thing that I'm going to ask you to do is describe what your roles are in this institution. So don't worry about Sam for minute, just tell us what you do, what your job titles are and how it's panning out.

Mentor

My role is as a learning mentor and support so Sam is one of my mentees and I'm here to pick up on behavioural issues, any personal issues, I need to refer to other agencies, also here to give him classroom support.

Interviewer

How long have you been doing this with Sam?

Mentor

Since February. (Three months.)

I'm actually an instructor which is not normal teaching, we do things like crafts, PE sessions, motor vehicle lessons. We do mentoring and we try and look after general pastoral care, type of things really.

Interviewer

And how long have you known Sam?

Mentor

From the first day he arrived, back in September.

Interviewer

What I'm going to ask you to do, each in turn, is just to describe the Sam you know. You can describe it in terms of his family, you can describe it in terms of his personality, but just paint us the picture of the Sam that you know.

Mentor

Sam has a big physical presence. He's very loud, quite outspoken. The Sam that I know, I believe he is actually quite gentle inside and he uses his physical presence to maybe intimidate or to just hold court with his peers and maybe staff. But I find him to be a generally pleasant individual that's got into the habit of performing and using his size and his loudness to put up a front, but, yes I think he's a big guy but maybe emotionally and mentally he's much younger than his size and age would suggest.

Interviewer

Thank you – what do you know of his family?

Mentor

I know he lives with his mum and that he's got older brothers. I know he sees his dad, dad has involvement with him. I've spoken to his mum on several occasions and she's very supportive of him trying to engage him with school. Dad also has a good relationship with Sam, but I know that dad tends to have maybe a little bit more influence over Sam's behaviour and decision-making than mum.

Interviewer

Tell me your perceptions of him.

Mentor

I met Sam at interview which was the school open evening when the parents came in, introduced the students, signed the paperwork, things like that. Very quiet then, sat at the back of the hall. Went over and had a conversation with him because, as Len said, he's quite a big lad. He is for his age. He's chunky, very fit and he seemed quite quiet then. He came to school. He was 100% attendance right the way through, no problem at all, bit of banter and then he sort of went childish and he's very, very childish. And then he comes back up into the adult world and then goes back out, and in, and out, and in, and out. And sometimes you just don't know which mood he's in, which way he's going to behave.

He does use his size to intimidate and his loudness, he shouts quite a lot, especially at the other students, his peers. But if you ever look, he'll come really close to you, he loves attention, he craves attention. If you tell him to back off, he backs off, but he does very, very silly little baby things to get your attention. He'll blow in your ear or just give your hairs a little pull on your arm to give him attention. He craves attention.

Physically he's fit, very fit, but he won't attempt PE lessons. He'll play football up the park, but he will not attend any official PE lessons. We used to take him to the Stables, which is an outdoor activity centre type of thing. We booked community transport and lo and behold daddy's driving the bus! So you've got daddy at the front, him being really quiet in the back and us of course going to the Stables. Needless to say, that's all stopped because he didn't want to have contact with his dad while he's with his peers.

Like I say, mum's quite supportive. Dad, I wouldn't say a lot, not too much. He's quite, sort of, shuts him off, cuts him dead, doesn't speak that much, all the rest of it and yet Sam seems to want to see him. He wants to understand what's going on. But his dad I think just cuts him dead when he's at work, and obviously when he's at school he's completely different too. And he acts differently to other people anyway, you can tell that.

There was one conversation that I had with Sam which was about his hobby. It expressed a real passion for his hobby, which was fishing. I spoke to him regarding that type of thing and he is of competition level. His attitude is totally and utterly different to anything else in his life, towards his fishing. He can do that for five hours, concentrate. I do a lot of competition stuff myself and when we spoke to Terry it was regarding this type of thing, and Terry was amazed that the kid can sit and not do anything apart from use his head and be controlled, not speak to anybody, just do what he's got to do. It's just amazing. I understand the way Sam got there, because I do competition stuff myself, so I understand what you have to put yourself through to concentrate for five hours in wind and rain and snow and everything, not speak to anybody and concentrate for that length of time, how physically demanding it is and mentally demanding, which is surprising with a kid who behaves the same way as he does.

I know where he comes from, I know a lot of the kids that he hangs about with and the areas that he hangs about in. I'm very surprised that he's not into drugs, I am very, very surprised because he's a smoker and it's one of those things that they do at that age. And the kids he hangs about with do, so I'm surprised that he doesn't do that.

Interviewer

Back to the fishing – have you fished with him for five hours, is it something you've taken him to?

Mentor

I'd love to. I would love to take him for five hours. I would do. No problem at all. I wouldn't have any qualms about talking Sam fishing at all. In fact he'd love it, he'd absolutely adore it. I even tried giving him little things which are fish related, as like 'well done' stickers and that seemed to work, but I think a lot of people started using it and it just failed then. If it was left quite small, it was controllable.

Interviewer

Can I ask you to bring to mind the last encounter you had with him, or something fairly recently? Just describe to me what you actually do with him.

Mentor

Well, I tend to speak to him on the telephone in terms of encouraging him to come into the centre to attend, because attendance is a big issue with Sam and when he's here I tend to shadow him in his lessons, so support him maybe help him with the work or keep him focused whilst the teacher's working with the rest of the class. The last conversation was regarding an incident that happened when Sam was leaving the school, so at the moment he's slightly vulnerable and not wanting to be at the centre, so I offered to be a support to him, to meet him and to go back with him to the bus stop to just make sure he's safe. I think our relationship's gone from who are you, why are you here, to actually thank you very much for caring but I don't really want it.

Interviewer

Just tell me about the incident.

Mentor

Sam was leaving the centre and was walking back to the bus stop and was approached by a number of youths from the area and they said to him that they didn't like the way he was walking, he was being provocative in his attitude and he replied, this is the way I walk and they threatened him, if you're in the high street on our turf, kind of thing, then we're going to hurt you, we're going to do something to you. So Sam's mum had the police involved, I've spoken to his mum and Sam himself and I guess he perceives that as a threat, a real risk to him, so we want to aid him to feel confident to be able to come to school and not be put off by those individuals who are threatening him.

Interviewer

Is he involved with the police in any other format?

Mentor

As far as I know, no. He's not in any trouble in any other context.

Interviewer

OK – was it the same with you? Talk through a typical interaction you've had with Sam.

Mentor

A typical interaction with Sam would be, first you go through the proviso of 'he's bigger than me' type of thing. Then you'll have the usual telling me to shut up and putting his chest up to me and walking up to me, that sort of thing. You just have to break it down and ask general questions, what's happening. He comes back down then and he talks quite normal, very short span but he does talk quite normal and then he just decides then, that's enough, and goes off on one. Starts shouting. He likes a relationship, he loves the fact no one spoke down to him when he first came, talked to him as an adult and his relationship with me is 'I can always go to him, to talk when I want his attention'. He loves that but he can't have it all the time, obviously. He would have it all the time, no doubt of that, he'd talk to me all day. He'd talk the biggest rubbish you've ever heard, but he'd talk all day. He does do his work, but you have to badger him constantly. He will do it, as long as he's with the right person.

Interviewer

Both of you – what do you think is going to happen to him? If we repeated this interview in one year or two years time, what do you think we'll be seeing with Sam?

Mentor

I think a lot depends on Sam really because as a mentor I'm trying to get into him looking at himself, his behaviour in certain settings, school, outside of school, in relationships with his mum, his dad, his peers, but also future wise. Identifying his skills, maybe some ambitions and putting some sort of plan together, what do you want to become and how do you want to work at it. And I guess he doesn't have the maturity to even want to discuss and open a conversation on that level. He'd rather say I don't know and put it off and not think about it for now. So in a year's time I'd say the situation would be the same but on the other hand the question should be saying 'Are we here at the centre providing adequate needs and support for Sam and have we identified those needs correctly?'

School-wise he's going to be exactly the same as he is this year – he's never going to change, never. If you read the file, all the agencies from birth I think who have been involved with Sam and his mum, everybody's tried and everybody's gone through the normal everyday route that we always go down. It works to a very, very thin line, it works, but then it doesn't, then it does, then it doesn't. And that's happened all the way through the kid's life, it's all there, put it all together, the parents have had it, they've had this programme, that programme, involved with this agency, that agency. So mum's tried, dad's tried, all the agencies have tried. There's only one person who hasn't and that's Sam. Sam, he plays, it's a play. It's playtime. When he leaves school, I've got visions of him working market stalls, humping stuff around the market stall, that type of thing, where his interaction with people is fast, because that's what he likes. And he can hold centre stage when he's on a market stall. That's what I think he'll do. I think he'll just mess about till about 17 or 18 and then the penny might drop. I don't think it will, but it might, you never know.

8

Themes, Observations and Applications

Themes

We have taken a phenomenological approach to researching school exclusion. This approach was described in the Introduction to Part 2. Our main concern in adopting this approach to research was to preserve the accounts of the key players involved in an exclusion. Therefore, complex and detailed data analysis has not been carried out because it is not our purpose to use the case examples to suggest causes or issues which could be generalised to other situations. In any case, the purposive sampling method and small number of cases are not conducive to making generalisations.

We have followed the guidance from Giorgi (1994) in attempting to carry out some analysis (or as Groenewald, 2004, describes it, explicitation) of the data. This section comprises what Giorgi terms the '*search for essences*'.

An intensive process of reading, re-reading and reflection has led us to identify two major themes, or essences: family circumstances and support. The reason for identifying just two is that, for these themes, it was possible to highlight occurrences at two levels. Firstly, there was consistency across case examples. Both themes were highlighted in all five examples. Secondly, there was consistency within case examples. Some element of each theme was identified by more than one contributor in each case example.

Both themes are discussed below. In these sections we have discussed the themes in relation to the stability/instability and psychodynamic perspectives introduced in Chapters 1 and 2. In addition, we have considered how far these themes can be linked to current literature and research about exclusion.

Family circumstances

In all cases, there was a family circumstance or set of circumstances that was considered to have played a part in the young person's difficulties. All of the case examples were single parent families. In two cases, domestic violence (witnessed by the young person) had been a factor in the family breakdown.

Exclusion from school is one of a range of negative outcomes for children that are associated with adverse family circumstances (for example, see Vulliany and Webb, 2001; Mason and Prior, 2008). In their interviews of young men convicted of gun crime, Hayden *et al* (2008) comment: 'with a few notable exceptions, interviews with the offenders in this study illustrated that they had grown up in disrupted family environments, had underachieved, had been excluded from mainstream education and had poor work histories in legitimate employment' (p167).

It is important to emphasise that the relationship between family circumstances and exclusion is not a straightforward one of cause and effect; it cannot be argued that adverse family circumstances will inevitably lead to exclusion. There are two possible ways of understanding this relationship. Firstly, as Vulliany and Webb (2001) argue, there is the notion of social construction of exclusion. One of the factors in difficult behaviour, exclusion and other associated problems is not just home circumstances, but problems that these might generate in interactions between home and school.

Secondly, the behaviour challenges that might result in exclusion are not absolutes. By this, Vulliany and Webb mean that different schools will differently construe what constitutes a problem. Whether behaviour is difficult enough to warrant exclusion, therefore, is mediated by the social context in which it occurs, thus leading to varying tolerance levels between schools. Differing constructions might be reflected in the way in which exclusion is handled. Some schools, for example, use unofficial exclusion such as sending a pupil home to cool down, or suggesting that the pupil moves to another school, thereby avoiding any formal record of a fixed term or permanent exclusion. In contrast, other schools will use the formal sanction of exclusion.

Chapter 1 introduced the notion of unstable systems as a means of understanding exclusion. The case examples all give a picture of families that are either undergoing a period of significant instability or have done so in the past. Often, the point at which the child's difficulties first became apparent coincided with a period of family instability:

> It was around the same time as me and her dad split up so I don't know if that has any bearing on her behaviour, I personally think it has. (Letitia's mother).

> Looking back now it wasn't a life, I was just existing really. (Chip's mother)

> There's a whole lot of background stuff that we know about and we were informed about. The conflict between mum and dad and the fact that all the sisters were either at home or not at home. All that sort of stuff. (Head teacher of school that excluded Jack)

> Sam has, on a few occasions, been upset and said it's his dad's fault for the way he is and if his dad hadn't have left everything would have been OK ... but we could not just stop together because it just wasn't working. (Sam's mother)

If an unstable family system is recognised as a factor in the pupil's difficulties, the education system sometimes seeks support for the family via a referral to other agencies that might provide help and support. However, the very instability that prompts the referral can then lead to non-attendance at appointments. Thus a cycle is set up of referral, non-attendance and subsequent discharge with the outcome that the family does not receive support and indeed is likely to become labelled as a family that is 'unsupportive' or 'hard to reach'. In the case examples this is reflected in some issues about non-attendance with a variety of agencies, or the pupil's non-attendance at the school or PRU. However, the perspective on non-attendance from the point of view of Leitia's mother is interesting to consider:

> ....things were getting worse at Primrose High School. In fact I was keeping her off school some days. If I thought 'today she's gonna get in trouble' I didn't send her.

In other words, not sending Letitia to school was a means of avoiding trouble, a coping mechanism. This has parallels in the disease control model outlined in the Introduction to Part 1.

The difficulties created by being part of an unstable system are then exacerbated when intervention systems are based on expectations that are rooted in stability and linear change:

> There were all sorts of rewards set up, negotiated targets with him. Things that were there for example (shows me a reward chart) for example in 2006, October 2006, which was the year that it sort of started. But there would be times that he did well all morning ... A lot of the time he'd be in class to begin with but as soon as he started playing up or not wanting to do it, or disrupting or going around hitting other children.' (Head teacher, Jack's case example)

What is interesting is that all the schools mention family circumstances as a factor in the pupil's difficulties, but none go on to say how they either took account of these circumstances in dealing with the pupil or how they took active steps to support the family. The difficulties are mentioned by way of explaining the problems, but overall there is a rather defeatist feeling that the family circumstances are so overwhelmingly adverse that there is little that can be done to change things. For example, in Chip's case, the Family Support Worker who has had opportunities to work with the family refers to the possibility of a residential placement.

Although our case examples all have unstable and chaotic family backgrounds, we could just as easily have picked another five examples of similarly adverse circumstances where the pupil was not excluded from school. Why should this be the case?

Part of the answer lies in the social construction of behaviour already discussed: the particular school environment that the pupil finds him or herself in will play a large part in determining whether the behaviour challenges lead to exclusion or not. Jull (2008) is quite forthright in his statement that: 'forcible removal and confinement of a child for non-compliance remains an indication of failure on the part of the school and the education system to resolve problems linked to behaviour' (p14). We come back to the differences in interaction between home and school as a factor, rather than the adverse circumstances per se. In these cases, some form of mediation or intervention might be helpful, as is the case in Vulliany and Webb's research (2001). The Home Office funded project that they evaluated involved the provision of a home/school worker described as 'acting as an intermediary'. However there are other factors that can be suggested in addition to the interaction with the school system. Notions of risk and resilience are helpful in seeing how some children and families cope with adverse circumstances. In these cases, there are elements of resilience that balance out the risk factors. These ideas will be explored further later in this chapter when we look at Macdonald and O'Hara's (1998) ten element model of mental health.

Support

The issue of support came up time and again in the case examples. In some cases, extracts were identified as being related to support because they discussed resources. In others, support was identified in terms of requests for support. The issue of resources was viewed differently by parents and schools. Schools tended to cite lack of resources and support as a factor outside their control. For example, the head teacher in Jack's case example refers to a shortage of PRU places. The LSU manager in Sam's case example comments that access to offsite education at an earlier stage would have been helpful, so here it is not simply shortage of resources but not having access to resources. Interestingly, one finding from Pavey and Visser's study (2003) was that head teachers sometimes used the threat of exclusion as a means of securing resources from the Local Authority.

We would argue that school's view of support and resources, as reflected in our case examples, are illustrative of Solomon's discussion of evacuation in chapter 2. When asked to reflect on the pupil's exclusion and how it might have been prevented, schools often mention off-site provision (for example, via increased access to PRU or vocational placements) as a means of prevention. It could be argued, therefore, that the unconscious process of evacuation is a driver behind the suggestion that the way to prevent exclusion is to resource other types of exclusion; that is, the 'other'. These 'other' provisions essentially remove the pupil from the setting where the 'bad feelings' are being experienced. Thus the pupil is rendered invisible, but in a way that is construed by schools as being in the pupil's best interests. Exclusion, therefore, can be interpreted in two ways: as an action that involves a set of procedures and protocols, or as an overarching epistemology that drives policy and practice at a number of levels (individual, school, local authority). The influence of the latter is more difficult to trace, since it might involve the unconscious processes of evacuation referred to earlier and might be made acceptable through the talking up of off-site provision as a positive intervention. This dual view of exclusion is hinted at by Gray and Panter (2000). Lee and Breen (2007) reflect this idea when they describe the caring approach taken by schools, based on notions of the common good. Fulfilling the common good, however, means that some pupils are excluded because their presence affects the wellbeing and progress of the majority of those in the system. Here then we have exclusion seen as a benign act, a type of positioning that Solomon refers to in his psychodynamic perspective.

Parental views about resources tended to focus on deployment, expressing the view that schools had resources and support but chose not to use them for their child. For example, Letitia's mother commented specifically that the school refused to pay for a mentoring service that had previously been successful. Two other case examples refer to schools being reluctant to pay for mentoring, or only being able to fund mentoring for a set period of time. Many of the contributors across all case examples make positive reference to the role of mentors in terms of support; for example:

> Anything that happened in the week I could go back to her [the mentor] and she would speak about it with me and then talk to the teachers after and it would be sorted. (Letitia)

> ...but I think what it is because he has got a mentor as well, Len, I think Len is literally bending over backwards for Sam to keep him in there. (Sam's mother)

> So there's not enough help in the school ... Mentors should be in every school ... in that year Jack has blossomed and he's done a lot more in a year than he's done in three years at that school. (Jack's mother).

Discussions about resources were sometimes mentioned in the context of systems failure. Both parents and educational establishments comment that access to resources was sometimes slow or not forthcoming at all due to difficulties such as lost or missing paperwork. Systems failure was therefore identified as an element of the support theme. Two of the cases (Jack and Letitia) make specific reference to difficulties such as lost or mixed up paperwork, which resulted in a longer wait than was necessary for school placement following exclusion. Jack's head teacher talks about waiting for a PRU place for a pupil, only to be told that the places had been filled by other pupils deemed to be a higher priority. Unrecognised special educational needs could also be viewed as a systems failure. In some of the case examples, there were clear learning needs which had not been addressed. For example, David's mother tells how she kept saying that he had language and communication difficulties, but she was not listened to:

> I know David had severe communication difficulties which was expressed to the school, it wasn't picked up on ... one [advisory teacher] has told me that David wanted more attention from his mum which I disagreed with.....again I told them I've got issues with his communication difficulties in which they disagreed ... they said no they hadn't noticed anything like that.

In Chip's case, his mother requested a statutory assessment of his special educational needs, having been advised to do so by the PRU. It is interesting that the PRU did not make this request, but left the responsibility for doing so with a very vulnerable parent. However, she did make contact with Parent Partnership, who supported her, but even this support could not prevent systems failure:

> I helped mum draft a letter to make that request to the SEN Team and she hand delivered it but for some reason it wasn't received and things became a little bit messy so we had to pick things up again later on in September.' (Parent Partnership, Chip).

Requests for support were principally found in parent's accounts, in the context of asking for support but not receiving any. Letitia's mother recounts asking for counselling and David's mother comments that she repeatedly told his Primary School that he was experiencing communication difficulties, but these concerns were not followed up and were attributed to the family circumstances. Letitia mentions the lack of support in school and the fact that the one source of support was from a member of staff who did not actually have any responsibilities in relation to Letitia. Lack of support was one of the memories about mainstream schooling in Hornby and Witte's study of adults who had been placed in residential special schools (Hornby and Witte, 2008).

The issues raised by the support theme might be summed up via this comment by the representative from the Parent Partnership Service in Chip's case: 'the miracle question would be that ... he'd have the support that he needs...' It is a great pity that receiving appropriate support is seen as part of a miracle.

Observations

Improvement in behaviour and attendance at school remains a concern for many education authorities. Initiatives such as Behaviour and Education Support Teams (BESTs) have provided a range of group and individual programmes that address some of the holistic factors leading to difficulties within school. Evaluation by Halsey, Gulliver, Johnson, Martin and Kinder (2005) identified BESTs as having a positive impact on children with regard to attainment, attendance, behaviour and wellbeing. Positive impacts on staff included an increased understanding of emotional difficulties and developing strategies to cope with children presenting with emotional difficulties. Provision of early intervention strategies appears to have a huge part to play in reducing exclusion rates.

A number of current legislation documents recognise the importance of education in enabling children and young people to reach their emotional health and occupational capacities. Every Child Matters (Department for Education and Skills, 2003) states that one of its aims is 'to ensure that every child has the chance to fulfil their potential by reducing levels of educational failure' (Every Child Matters, Executive Summary, p6). One of the five outcomes recommends enjoying and achieving. However, we need fully to recognise and acknowledge that individual children have differing strengths and weaknesses; some are academically more able, whilst others thrive using more practical, hands-on skills. Curriculum planning and provision should reflect this. Children and young people should not be made to feel failures if they do not achieve specific SAT levels. These may not reflect their capabilities in other areas.

As the head teacher in Jack's case example suggests,

> There are more vocational courses and courses geared for boys of this nature who have some benefit from a more practical, more vocational approach to work. It is coming but we seem to have gone full circle in that respect over the years where I know in other countries you get to a point where you're going off on an academic route or you're going off to do something more practical and learn a trade. Where we've sort of lost that in this country, I think it's something that we need to get back because the children haven't changed in that profile. Not everybody can go down that academic route and I think everybody has been pushed down that route and everyone is deemed a failure if you don't get five A to C grades at GCSE. And lots of them won't but they'll be able in years to come, come and fix your plumbing that's gone wrong. But we're not pushing them in that direction. We're not helping them to get there and that's where the problems come. And certainly when they get to high school, they seem to get earlier and earlier in the junior schools, where for lots of reasons, where there is dysfunctionality in the home. Whether it's the fact they're not academic, whether it's the fact they're seeing or being exposed to many more things that perhaps they shouldn't be. That they're becoming disillusioned with school, not enjoying and not doing what they need to be doing to get that basis before they go to high school. And when they get there it's still the same pressure towards, to do these types of lessons. Well, some of the children won't and for whatever reason that's kicked them off the pathway, they still need to find some route and I think some of them won't find other routes and until things come, things like a more personalised curriculum.

Every Child Matters – the Green Paper (Department for Education and Skills, 2003) proposes that more emphasis is needed on preventative strategies. Establishing ways of increasing children's self esteem and motivation within educational settings will help their willingness to attempt tasks they perceive as more onerous. Fostering a sense of achievement in some areas will reduce feelings of inadequacy and encourage self-belief in others.

Every Child Matters also recommends, 'developing on the spot service delivery' (Executive Summary, p9). The case examples presented here may have benefited from this approach. Early identification of children at risk of exclusion coupled with timely, appropriately placed interventions may reduce the need for dealing with difficult behaviour that has further evolved due to a lack of understanding or assistance. Waiting times for services can mean that children's emotional health and well-being deteriorates during the delay in accessing services. Proactive strategies and approaches aimed at recognising the impact of life events on children's emotional well-being would ensure that those individuals do not suffer further due to punitive adult reactions following misunderstandings about their behavioural presentation. We are all too often unaware of the events unfolding in the personal lives of our pupils.

Targeted support and resources often appear to be lacking or vastly over-subscribed, sometimes leading to changes in their referral criteria. Schools that wish to offer specialised interventions are often unable to do so due to their own financial constraints and conflicting demands. School resources being utilised to pay for support for an individual child mean that those monies cannot be spent elsewhere. This could lead to resentment toward that child. As the case examples also suggest, it is difficult to offer what may be perceived as special treatment for one child and not to others in their class. Similarly, peers may begin to believe that they need to act inappropriately in order to achieve what they perceive as the rewards of their classmate.

Head teacher:

> So I would go out with them and I would do stuff but because you were a teacher taking them out you set things up. So one day you played football, one day you'd play games. So it was great for them to be in that group with the deputy head, so other children would want to be in it therefore they'd play up to see if they could get in and you've got to try. Some of these children needed it from a nurturing point of view to know how to cope in football if you get tackled, it doesn't mean a fight, it means you get up and get on with it. And how to cope with somebody swearing at you because you've missed the goal; that's not a fight and that's what we were trying to teach them, but the downside, and it worked for these individuals, the downside was there's a lot of children who are on the periphery who may raise their heads and become difficult to control or discipline. They saw that as 'it's not fair' and I think that's part of the problems that these children learn and they seem that way to parents as well, as to be getting all the rewards and the rewards that their children aren't getting and their children are behaving well.

> And you have to have a balance between that and not doing too much of that because then with children you'll get to the point when they'll only do it if they get something special.

Risk and Resilience

A number of key factors have been identified which place children at higher risk of developing emotional and behavioural problems. These are commonly split into headings of:

- factors in the person
- factors in the family
- factors in the school/community
- factors in the wider world

Daniel and Wassell (2002)

It is conceivable that there is a fifth set of factors, that is those of 'Factors in professional engagement'. There are a number of ways in which the behaviour and agenda of professionals engaged with children and their families can impact on their resilience when faced with adverse circumstances. For example, we need to take greater responsibility for the welfare of children and not be passing referrals from one agency to another (playing the pass the parcel game, as described in chapter 1) in order to cope with our own limited resources and meet increasingly shorter waiting time deadlines. There is a real need to increase joined-up working and communication between agencies and not simply pay lip-service to the idea. For example, forging greater links between Child and Adolescent Mental Health Services (CAMHS) and education services, since emotional well-being has a recognisable impact on educational attainment and vice versa.

In Chapter 1 we discuss the need for services to guard against playing games with referrals. It is all too easy to play the pass the parcel game by announcing that a different service is more appropriate for the needs of the family concerned. Both services may have valuable interventions to offer individually, but if they worked together they could impact on later re-referral of families. Children do not develop in isolation from their environments; their home lives impact upon their school lives and vice versa. Multi-agency working can address some of these complexities, offering strategies that incorporate the demands and expectations of several environments rather than looking at home, school and the community as separate entities. As Solomon suggests in chapter 2, 'genuine multi-agency practice' might enable pupil's needs to be met.

Bronfenbrenner's Ecological Systems theory (1979) considers the way in which children's development is affected by the complex system of relationships within their wider environment. The microsystem incorporates those structures with the most direct contact with a child such as their family and school. The mesosystem forms the connection between the structures within the microsystem, for example the connection between child and teacher. The exosystem looks at the impact of wider aspects of the social system, including mass media and the community. Whilst the macrosystem concerns the cultural and legal factors which cascade through the other layers, changes within one layer can and do have a profound effect within another. Child development is believed to be influenced by the experiences they have within the settings they spend most time in. For example, children may model their behaviour on that of the adults they are close to. If adults demonstrate listening in a nurturing manner, children may copy.

Similarly, MacDonald and O'Hara (1998) propose a ten-element mental health promotion and demotion model. They suggest how areas of intervention can impact upon our well-being at an individual (micro), group (meso), community (macro) and national (exo) level. By pairing risk and protective factors, it is possible to identify strategies for intervention, for example using activities to promote social participation may reduce the child's experience of social alienation. Some of these issues have attracted a national audience and we outline some of these below.

National Institute of Clinical Excellence guidelines

It is clear that the emotional health of children and young people has a profound effect on their ability to cope with the demands of the school day. Children's mental health difficulties such as depression and anxiety will impact on their concentration and retention of information, whilst some pupils may feel so worried about the safety of family members that they seemingly develop school-phobia, presenting with severe anxiety that thwarts their attempts to attend school. (Some may even manipulate their school behavioural policy in order to be sent home.)

In 2008, the National Institute for Clinical Excellence (NICE) issued formal guidance for promoting the social and emotional wellbeing of children in primary education. Recommendations suggested that primary schools adopt a comprehensive, whole school approach to children's social and emotional wellbeing. Practitioners working in primary education should also be trained to identify and assess early signs of emotional distress and children at risk of developing behavioural problems. Guidelines regarding the promotion of social and emotional wellbeing in secondary education are under development and due to be available in early 2009.

Prior to children becoming at risk of exclusion primarily due to factors of emotional health and wellbeing, it is hoped that difficulties can be identified and dealt with before becoming more severe and entrenched, possibly needing greater levels of intervention. Greater understanding of the impact of emotional health on educational attainment may also serve to allow more leniencies when dealing with children experiencing difficult life events.

Greater emphasis might be needed on parental support. All too often parents appear to be contacted by schools when something has gone wrong. For parents who have already experienced their own difficulties within the education system, this can feel particularly punitive.

Department of Children, Schools and Families

In October 2008, there was an announcement of pilot projects to support those at risk of exclusion. These included new and innovative ways of teaching. Alternative teaching methods are suggested prior to children becoming disaffected rather than as a provision once they have been excluded. For example establishing enterprise-focused extended learning centres and increasing work-placement opportunities.

DCSF *Exclusion Guidance* (2007) states that head teachers should be able to refer pupils at risk to other agencies, alternative or additional provision. This relies on there being places available at these provisions. Staff training should also be established to 'promote good behaviour and prevent poor behaviour'.

Two-thirds of excluded pupils have been identified as having special educational needs (SEN). This suggests a need for more specific provision for some pupils. 'Early identification and intervention, accurate assessment and the arrangement of appropriate provision to meet pupil's SEN usually leads to better outcomes.' (DCSF *Exclusion Guidance*, 2007, pt 2, p53). It is possible that the specific needs of these pupils are not being met. They may not understand the work or simply what is being asked of them, leading to disruptive behaviour. If academic work was set within the capabilities of each child then perhaps fewer behavioural difficulties would be observed. Earlier identification of literacy/numeracy difficulties would also ensure that children's academic needs are met sooner.

Schools may not yet be fully aware that their interventions form part of the comprehensive CAMHS (Child and Adolescent Mental Health Service) model at Tier One level. All teaching staff have responsibility in regard to the mental wellbeing of the children and young people they work with.

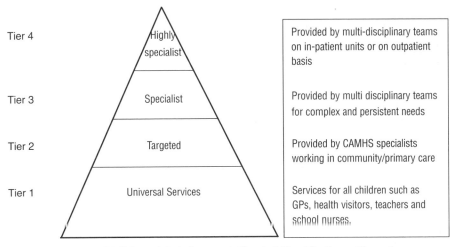

Figure 8.1: The Child and Adolescent Mental Health Four Tiered Approach

Social and Emotional Aspects of Learning (SEAL) approach

A number of excluded pupils may experience difficulties in their social skill development, ability to problem-solve and work as part of a team. The SEAL (Social and Emotional Aspects of Learning, Department for Education and Skills, 2005) programme focuses on five components: self-awareness, managing feelings, motivation, empathy and social skills. The materials aid development of group-working, understanding others' perceptions, conflict resolution and promoting resilience. This is potentially an excellent preventative measure. Although early indicators may suggest that implementation needs to be consistent and used across the whole school, it has the potential to reduce exclusions through greater awareness of pupils' social and emotional needs.

Alternative Education

It is the remit of Pupil Referral Units to provide suitable education for excluded pupils (and those being taught beyond school for other reasons). Suitable education is defined as 'efficient education suitable to age, ability, aptitude and to any special educational needs' (*Every Child Matters*, DfES, 2003). If education programmes were more individualised to fit the ability and aptitude of pupils within mainstream settings there might be less need for exclusion.

The focus of PRUs is also to enable pupils to re-access mainstream schooling as quickly as possible. Yet often the provision of education in these units is different with smaller staff-pupil ratios and a more practical curriculum. Mainstream educators could learn from these approaches.

The development of school league tables is placing academic achievement high on the school agenda. An unintended consequence of this is that it favours the academically successful. Less academically successful pupils are unfavourably viewed and disruptive pupils perceived as a risk to the rest of the school.

Complexity

Factors leading to exclusion are clearly complex.

'*Better outcomes for the most excluded*' (Schneider, 2007) suggests reducing exclusion rates by 'engaging vulnerable young people at transition', providing early intervention when needs have been identified and promoting zero exclusion policies within statutory provision (Schneider, 2007). It also recognises the potential benefit in restoring missing protective factors such as skill development and providing praise and encouragement. Projects run by organisations such as NACRO aim to 'provide disengaged young people the opportunity to learn new skills'. Programmes offer vocational training such as bricklaying and car mechanics, but also address social skills and literacy/ numeracy development.

The Steer report *Learning Behaviour* (DfES 2005) recognises the importance of parents and schools working together to maintain good behaviour. Increasing levels of parental engagement with schools is a key objective. However, the report also recognises the challenge of overcoming the impact of the negative experiences that some parents had in their own education.

Indicators for future work

Chapter 1 describes work mapping risk factors which are associated with children and young people who have been permanently excluded from school. They can be considered additive. If a child has more than five, there appears to be a high probability that the child will be excluded from school before Year 10. Of note is the fact that only one of the factors has anything to do with education (Pitchford, 2006)

The risk factors are defined thus:

1. Child is known to CAMHS (mental health services)
2. Child is on the special educational needs register (SEN)
3. Child is Looked After by the Local Authority (LAC)
4. Child is looked after by a single parent
5. Child is looked after by a disabled parent

6. Child's household has reports of domestic violence
7. Child has a child protection plan (used to be called child protection register)
8. Child has no fixed abode or is sleeping rough
9. Child is at risk of sexual exploitation

   Child's parent is:
10. rejecting the child
11. misusing substances
12. known to mental health services.
13. reporting behaviour management problems with the child.

Total = 13

In a pilot study a secondary school screened all of their children for these risk factors at the beginning of Year 8. In the first cycle of this, there were seven children with more than five risk factors. By the end of the year, none of these seven were still within the school. Not all had been formally excluded. Some had merely been recommended to find another school. However, the model had identified children unlikely to complete their education in that setting.

In the second year, the same exercise was undertaken. Six children were identified as having three or more risk factors. Two pupils had five and two pupils had six. Information obtained the following January suggested that one of the girls who had initially been thought of as having five, actually had seven. Drug use and unstable housing were not known when the original screen was completed. All of the children identified were targeted for at least two interventions:

- Their parents were invited to meet the school's psychologist and pastoral head. At this meeting, the nature of the screen was explained and the parents invited to keep in touch with the school if things became difficult with the pupil

- The children were all given BLOGs (weB LOGs) within the school computer system. When the children were excluded from a class, they were invited to write their account of what happened in their BLOG. Access to the BLOG was restricted to the individual pupil, the psychologist and the teacher who ran the Learning Support Unit in the school. The BLOG was intended to facilitate a different mode of communication between the pupil and the school. If children felt unfairly treated, they had a safe medium through which to express this, thus giving them a voice. The case examples offered in this book suggest levels of complexity not always appreciated by professional staff. Although not all the pupils engaged with telling their stories to the authors, the BLOG provided a more acceptable medium through which to communicate. Additionally, sitting at a computer screen could be calming after an incident in a class which resulted in the pupil being removed from the class. Furthermore the BLOG has the potential to empower the child. See chapter 2 for an analysis of the rationale used here.

By the end of the school year, none of the children had been excluded, although one had more or less stopped attending (the girl with seven risk factors). By October of the following year, the girl with seven risk factors had been permanently excluded and one of the boys with six risk factors was having a six week respite course in a local Pupil Referral Unit. The remaining four children were still in the school and the staff were of the opinion that they would stay there and avoid being excluded. This work is still in its early stages and will be evaluated formally in the future.

The focus of attention on the one child permanently excluded and the other one in the Pupil Referral Unit need not distract the staff in the school from celebrating their successes. Clearly it is unwise to generalise from such a small and unrepresentative sample, but the general principles are probably sound in that the school can celebrate success with the four children who have not been excluded, in spite of the complexities of their lives and high number of risk factors.

This book has set out to describe the immense complexities of the lives of children who become excluded from school. It is the authors' assertion that the exclusion itself adds to those complexities. Whilst it may be a solution for the school, it usually adds to the problems for the family and young person. By examining and documenting the contexts of these young people we have found increasing empathy with this client group. This can be communicated within the schools experiencing the difficulties which lead to exclusion. Often this changes the perceptions of the young people with a softening of attitude and increase in tolerance. If this book is successful in suggesting methods for reducing school exclusion, then the authors will be most content.

References

Arnold, C (2002) The dynamics of reading development. Unpublished thesis submitted for degree of PhD, University of Wolverhampton, UK

Arnold, C (2009) *We am NEET.* Presentation to the DECP conference. Worsley Park Hotel, Manchester January 2009. London: British Psychological Society

Arnold, E and Baldauf-Berdes, J (2002) *Maddalena Lombardini Sirmen – Eighteenth Century Composer, Violinist and Business Woman.* London: Scarecrow Press

Bazalgette, J (1989) *Young children becoming pupils.* London: The Grubb Institute.

Bion, W R (1962) A theory of thinking. In E.Bott-Spillius (ed) *Melanie Klein Today*, vol.1, London: Routledge

Bion, W R (1967) Attacks on linking. In *Second thoughts: selected papers on psychoanalysis.* London, Heinemann Medical (reprinted London, Maresfield Reprints, 1984)

Bowlby, J (1982) *Attachment.* 2nd edition of vol.1 Attachment and Loss. London: Hogarth Press

Bridgeland, M (1971) *Pioneer Work with Maladjusted Children.* London: Staples Press

British Educational Research Association (2004) *Revised Ethical Guidelines for Research.* Nottingham: British Educational Research Association

British Psychological Society (2004) *Guidelines for Minimum Standards of Ethical Approval in Psychological Research.* Leicester: British Psychological Society

Brofenbrenner, U (1979) *The Ecology of Human Development.* Cambridge, MA: Harvard University Press

Burt, C (1927) *The Young Delinquent.* London: University of London Press

Cooper, P (2004) Is 'inclusion' just a buzz-word? *Emotional and Behavioural Difficulties*, 9 (4) 219-222

Cooper, P (2005) Responding to SEBD: care or custody? *Emotional and Behavioural Difficulties*, 10 (1) 5-6

Daniel, B. and Wassall, S. (2002) *Assessing and Promoting Resilience in Vulnerable Children: Adolescence.* London: Jessica Kingsley

Davies, B and Harre, R (1990) Positioning: the discursive production of selves. *Journal for the Theory of Social Behaviour*, 20 (1) 43-63

Denscome, M (2003) *Good Research Guide: For Small Scale Research Projects.* Berkshire: McGraw Hill

Department for Children, Schools and Families (DCSF) (2008) *Back on Track: A Strategy for Modernising Alternative Provision for Young People.* London: HMSO

Department for Children, Schools and Families (October 2008) Ed Balls announces early support to keep pupils on track. London: Press notice 2008/0237

Department for Children, Schools and Families (2007) *Exclusion Guidance*. London HMSO

Department for Education and Skills (2003) *Every Child Matters*. London: HMSO

Department for Education and Skills (2005) *Excellence and Enjoyment: Social and Emotional Aspects of Learning*. Norwich: HMSO

Department for Education and Skills (2005) *Learning Behaviour: The Report of the Practitioner Group on School Behaviour and Discipline*. Norwich: HMSO

Dyson, S (2005) *Social Theory and Applied Health Research*. Berkshire: McGraw Hill

Education Act (1944) London: HMSO

Education Act (1981) London: HMSO

Festinger, L (1957) *A Theory of Cognitive Dissonance*. New York: Harper

Giorgi, A (1994) A phenomenological perspective on certain qualitative research methods. *Journal of Phenomenological Psychology*, 25(2) 190-220

Gray, P and Panter, S (2000) Exclusion or inclusion? A perspective on policy in England for pupils with emotional and behavioural difficulties. *Support for Learning*, 15(1) 4-7

Grimshaw, R (1994) *Educating Disruptive Children*. London: National Children's Bureau

Groenewald, T (2004) A phenomenological research design illustrated. *International Journal of Qualitative Methods*, 3(1) Article 4. Retrieved 2.11.2008 from http://www.ualberta.ca/~iiqm/back issues/3_1/pdf/groenewald.pdf

Halsey, K, Gulliver, C, Johnson A, Martin K and Kinder, K (2005) *Evaluation of Behaviour and Education Support Teams*. Slough: National Foundation for Educational Research

Hayden, C, Hales, G, Lewis,C and Silverstone, D (2008) Young men convicted of firearms offences in England and Wales: an exploration of family and educational background and opportunities for prevention. *Policy Studies*, 29(2) 163-178

Heidegger, M (1927) Sein und Zeit. Translated as *Being and Time* by John Macquarrie and Edward Robinson. Oxford: Basil Blackwell, 1978

Hoggett, P (2000) *Emotional life and the politics of welfare*. Basingstoke: Macmillan Press Ltd

Holmes, T and Rahe, R (1967) The Social Readjustment Rating Scale. *J Psychosom Res* 11(2): 213-8

Hornby, G and Witte, C (2008) Looking back at school-the views of adult graduates of a residential special school for children with emotional and behavioural difficulties. *British Journal of Special Education*, 35(2) 102-107

Husserl, E (1936) *Die Krisis der europäischen Wissenschaften und die transzentale Phäno-menologie: Eine Einleitung in die phänomenologische Philosophie (The Crisis of European Sciences and Transcendental Phenomenology: An Introduction to Phenomenological Philosophy)*. Translated by D Carr (1970). Evanston, IL: Northwestern University Press

Jull, S (2008) Emotional and behavioural difficulties (EBD): the special educational need justifying exclusion. *Journal of Research in Special Educational Needs*, 8(1) 13-18

Klein, M (1946) Notes on some schizoid mechanisms. *International Journal of Psycho-Analysis*, 27, 99-110

Klein, M (1959) Our adult world and its roots in infancy. *Human Relations*, 12, 291-303

Laslett, R, Cooper, P, Maras, P, and Rimmer, A (Eds) (1998) *Emotional and Behavioural Difficulties since 1945*. (The Association of Workers for Children with Emotional and Behavioural Difficulties)

Lawrence, G (1977) Management development ... some ideals, images and realities. In A.D. Colman and M.H.Geller (Eds.) *Group Relations Reader 2*. Washington DC: A.K.Rice Institute

Lee, T and Breen, L (2007) Young peoples' perceptions and experiences of leaving high school early: an exploration. *Journal of Community and Applied Social Psychology*, 17, 329-346

REFERENCES

Levering, B (2006) Epistemological issues in phenomenological research: how authoritative are people's accounts of their own perceptions? *Journal of Philosophy of Education*, 40(4) 451-462

Loehle, C (1995) Social barriers to pathogen transmission in wild animal populations. *Ecology* 1995, 76, p326-335

Lopez, K.A. and Willis, D.G. (2004) Descriptive versus interpretive phenomenology: their contribution to nursing knowledge. *Qualitative Health Research*, 14, 5, 726-735

MacDonald, G and O'Hara, K (1998) *Ten Elements of Mental Health, its promotion and demotion: Implications for practice*. Glasgow: Society of Health Education and Health Promotion Specialists

Marx, G (1959) *Groucho and Me*. New York: Da Capo Press

Mason, P and Prior, D (2008) The Children's Fund and the prevention of crime and anti-social behaviour. *Criminology and Criminal Justice*, 8(3) 279-296

Miller, E J and Rice, A K (1967) *Systems of Organization: The Control of Task and Sentient Boundaries*. London: Tavistock Publications. Reprinted in F Trist and H Murray (eds) The Social Engagement of Social Science, Vol. 1: The Socio-Psychological Perspective. London: Free Association Books, 1990

Miller, R L and Brewer, J D (Eds) (2003) *The A – Z of Social Research*. London: Sage

National Institute for Clinical Excellence (2008) *Emotional Health and Wellbeing in Primary School*

NCH (2007) *Literature Review – Resilience in Children and Young People*. London:NCH

Neill, A S (1962) *Summerhill*. London: Victor Gollancz

Obholzer, A (1996) Working in institutions. In C Jennings and E Kennedy (Eds.) *The Reflective Professional in Education: Psychological Perspectives on Changing Contexts*. London: Jessica Kingsley

Office for Standards in Education, Children's Services and Skills (Ofsted) (2007) *Pupil Referral Units: Establishing Successful Practice in Pupil Referral Units and Local Authorities*. London: HM Stationery Office

O'Hanlon, C and Thomas, G (2004) Editors' Preface. In D.Skidmore (Ed) *Inclusion*. Buckingham: Open University Press

Pavey, S and Visser, J (2003) Primary exclusions: are they rising? *British Journal of Special Education*, 30(4) 180-186

Pitchford, M (2006) *Secondary School Action Plan* (Personal Communication)

Rendall, S and Stuart, M (2005) *Excluded from School: Systemic Practice for Mental Health and Education Professionals*. London: Routledge

Roberts, V Z (1994). The organisation of work: contributions from open systems theory. In: A. Obholzer and V.Z.Roberts (eds.) *The Unconscious at Work: Individual and Organisational Stress in the Human Services*. London, Routledge

Ross, L (1977) The intuitive psychologist and his shortcomings: Distortions in the attribution process. In Berkowitz, L (ed) *Advances in Experimental Social Psychology*, Vol 10. New York: Academic Press

Rustique-Forrester, E (2001) Exploring teachers' perceptions of the causes, dynamics, and pressures of school exclusion: emerging findings from a small-scale study of four secondary schools. Forum: for Promoting 3-19 Comprehensive Education, 43(1) 43-47

Scanlon, C and Adlam, J (in press) Homelessness, dangerousness and disorder: the challenge of the anti-social and the societal response. In C Kaye and M Howlett (Eds.) *Roads to Recovery? The State of Mental Health Services Today and Tomorrow*. Oxford: Radcliffe Publishing

Schneider, J (2007) *Better outcomes for the most Excluded (Final Draft)*. London: Cabinet Office

Shaw, O (1965) *Maladjusted Boys*. London: George Allen and Unwin

Solomon, M (in press) Integrating reintegration: the role of child and adolescent mental health professionals in supporting the inclusion of excluded pupils. In R Harris, S Nashat and S Rendall (Eds.) *Promoting Psychological Well-being of Children and Young People in Educational Settings.* London: Karnac

Sprenkle, D H (Ed) (2005) *Research Methods in Family Therapy.* New York: Guilford Publications Inc

Steiner, J (1985) Turning a blind eye: the cover up for Oedipus. *International Review of Psycho-Analysis,* 12, 161-172

Stevens, R (1996) *Defining Social Psychology in Issues For Social Psychology.* Milton Keynes: Open University Press

Stubblefield, C and Murray, R (2002) A phenomenological framework for psychiatric nursing research. *Archives of Psychiatric Nursing,* XVI(4) 149-155

Sutoris, M (2000) Understanding schools as systems: implications for the management of pupil behaviour. *Educational and Child Psychology,* 17(1) 51-63

Todres, L and Wheeler, S (2001) The complementarity of phenomenology, hermeneutical existentialism as a philosophical perspective for nursing research. *International Journal of Nursing Studies,* 38, 1-8

Tredgold, A (1914) *Mental Deficiency* cited in Burt, C (1927) *The Young Delinquent.* London: University of London Press

Van Geert, P (1994) *Dynamic Systems of Development.* London: Harvester Wheatsheaf

Vulliany, G and Webb, R (2001) The social construction of school exclusion rates: implications for evaluation methodology. *Educational Studies,* 27(3) 357-370

Winnicott, D W (1971) *Playing and Reality.* Harmondsworth: Penguin

Winzer, M (1993) *The History of Special Education.* Washington DC: Gallaudet University Press

Index

Also from Trentham Books

September 2009

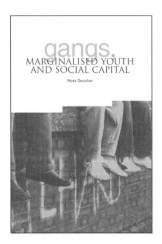

GANGS, MARGINALISED YOUTH AND SOCIAL CAPITAL

Ross Deuchar

Ross Deuchar's compelling research reveals the views of adolescents about their lives in the deprived areas of a large city, and the influence of gang culture and territoriality. The book features the voices of young people in Glasgow who have become disenfranchised by educational failure, unemployment and poverty and also of those who have overcome great challenges. The book examines the extent of their civic participation, social networks, reciprocity and trust, and presents case studies of projects and initiatives which are helping to re-engage young people.

Here is a book written for all those who work with young people from disadvantaged groups, whether in schools or youth organisations. It will be of particular relevance to academic researchers with an interest in social capital and also to community educationalists and youth leaders, secondary teachers and students who are studying towards qualifications in community education and youth work. The book will also interest people who are concerned with community welfare: politicians, the police, community sports development officers and youth coaches.

Dr Deuchar is senior lecturer in Education at the University of Strathclyde in Glasgow and the author of *Citizenship, Enterprise and Learning: harmonising competing educational agendas* (Trentham Books).

ISBN 978 1 85856 444 9, 192 pages, 234 x 156mm, £17.99

www.trentham-books.co.uk

FORTHCOMING FROM TRENTHAM BOOKS
October 2009

STRATEGIC ALTERNATIVES TO EXCLUSION FROM SCHOOL

Carl Parsons

Excluding children from school is not the only way to deal with unacceptable behaviour. It is the worst option for the excluded children, their families and society – but it is the easy option for the school.

Here is a book that shows how local authorities, working collaboratively with their schools and clusters, can dramatically reduce exclusions and make permanent exclusions unnecessary. And it shows how this is done. The lessons for all local authorities and schools are clear.

Professor Parsons' research in three low excluding local authorities and five high excluding local authorities recognises the challenges and barriers to a no-exclusions policy but clearly shows the way forward.

Strategic Alternatives to Exclusion from School fills the ground between school and national government, pointing to the responsibilities and powers that a supportive, challenging and conciliatory local authority has in respect of the education of all children. It sets out an agenda for action which is about enlisting full support from local authority counsellors and officers, building a shared commitment with schools, broadening what schools are able to offer, developing managed moves as a conciliatory and non punitive response, generating more alternative provision and developing multi-agency working, with greater involvement of the voluntary sector.

This is a book for everyone involved in managing the education of behaviourally challenging children and young people. It is of particular relevance to those working at the level of strategy and operation in local authority Children's Services departments and to managers in schools. And other services which receive school rejects will find the debates about appropriate provision of help in their work.

Carl Parsons is Professor of Education at Canterbury Christ Church University. He has researched school exclusions over a period of 15 years, taking a consistently cool and evidence based approach and a moral stance that school exclusion is a punitive device which creates social ills elsewhere.

ISBN 978 1 85856 464 7, 244 x 170mm, price £15.99

www.trentham-books.co.uk